MW00774903

POETRY AT WORK

glynn young

foreword by scott edward anderson

masters in fine living series

ts T. S. Poetry Press • New York

T. S. Poetry Press
Ossining, New York
Tspoetry.com

This book includes various references from or to the following brands & sources: Metropolitan Transit Authority; Poetry Society of America; Streetfare Journal, Transportation Displays Incorporated; LEGO is a trademark of the LEGO Group; PowerPoint, a Microsoft Office project, Microsoft Corporation; Johnson & Johnson and J&J; Nike; Google; Robert Mondavi Winery; Hartford Insurance Company; State Farm Insurance, State Farm is a trademark of State Farm Mutual Automobile Insurance Company; General Foods, now part of Kraft Foods Group; Kraft, known as Kraft Foods Group; Jell-O®, a registered trademark of Kraft Foods Group; TED, a copyright of TED Conferences, LLC; Lotus Notes evolved into IBM® Notes® and IBM Domino®, software products of IBM (Lotus, Domino and IBM are registered trademarks); Lincoln Benefit Life Company, now part of Allstate, which is a registered trademark; AT&T; Facebook; Twitter; YouTube; Edward Hopper's painting "Nighthawk"; The Art Institute of Chicago; NEA: National Endowment for the Arts; PBS: Public Broadcasting Service; EPA: Environmental Protection Agency; NSA: National Security Agency; TSA: Transportation Security Administration; Chicago Board of Trade; Department of Defense; *The Graduate* (movie by Mike Nicholls) (1967); *Isadora* (movie by Karl Reisz) (1968); *The Poetry of William Carlos Williams of Rutherford* by Wendell Berry, Counterpoint, 2011; *The Doctor Stories* by William Carlos Williams, New Directions, 2012; *Spring and All* by William Carlos Williams, New Directions Pearls (2013) Facsimile edition of 1923 original edition; "Crossing Brooklyn Ferry" by Walt Whitman; Dante's *Inferno*; *The Jungle* by Upton Sinclair, first published in book form by Doubleday in 1906.; *The Man in the Gray Flannel Suit* by Sloan Wilson, Simon and Schuster (1955); *The Embezzler* by Louis Auchincloss, Houghton Mifflin (1966); *Post Office* by Charles Bukowski, Black Sparrow Press (1971); *The Norton Anthology of Poetry*, W. W. Norton & Co. (2005); "Paradise Lost" by John Milton (1667); "Idylls of the King" by Alfred Lord Tennyson (1859-1885); *In Search of Excellence* by Tom J. Peters and Robert H. Waterman, Jr., Harper & Row (1982); *Iliad*; *Beowulf*, "The Love Song of J. Alfred Prufrock" by T.S. Eliot (1920); "Four Quartets" by T.S. Eliot; "Stopping by Woods on a Snowy Evening" by Robert Frost; *Official Entry Blank* by Ted Kooser, University of Nebraska Press (1969); *The Glass Children*, University of Georgia Press (1986); *Success Stories: Poems and Essays*, Limestone Books (1998) by Richard Cole; *Prose and Poetry of America*, edited by H. Ward, McGraw (1940); *England in Literature* (1963); "Fionn and the Salmon of Knowledge," an Irish folk tale; "The Tell-Tale Heart" by Edgar Allan Poe; "Paul Revere's Ride" and "The Song of Hiawatha" by Henry Wadsworth Longfellow; "If" by Rudyard Kipling; Mickey Mouse, Cinderella and Disney World, The Walt Disney Company.

"October Layoffs" by Robert Cole, from *Success Sotries: Poems and Essays*, Limestone Books, 1998, used with permission.

Cover image by Claire Burge claireburge.com

ISBN 978-0-9898542-9-0

Library of Congress Cataloging-in-Publication Data:
Young, Glynn
    [Nonfiction.]
    Poetry at Work/Glynn Young
    ISBN 978-0-9898542-9-0
    Library of Congress Control Number: 2013955106

To Janet, who's lived almost all of this with me

Table of Contents

Foreword 11

Introduction 17

Chapter 1: How to Recognize a Poet at Work 19
Poet Focus: William Carlos Williams 21

Chapter 2: The Poetry of the Interview 25
Poet Focus: Wallace Stevens 28

Chapter 3: The Poetry of the Workspace 31
Poet Focus: Dana Gioia 34

Chapter 4: The Poetry of the Commute 37
Poet Focus: Carl Sandburg 41

Chapter 5: The Poetry of the Boss 44
What Poetry Brings to Business 48

Chapter 6: The Poetry of Vision Statements 51
Poet Focus: Ted Kooser 55

Chapter 7: The Poetry of PowerPoint 57

Chapter 8: The Poetry of the Organization Chart 60

Chapter 9: The Poet in the Culture of Control................................63

Chapter 10: The Poetry of Beauty in the Workplace...................67

Chapter 11: The Poetry of Speechwriting.................................70

Chapter 12: The Poetry of Transparency.................................76

Chatper 13: The Poetry of the Crisis.......................................79

Chapter 14: The Poetry of Interpersonal Conflict.......................85
Take Your Poet to Work Day..89

Chapter 15: The Poetry of the Best Job You Ever Had
(Or the Worst)...92

Chapter 16: The Poetry of Unemployment...............................96

Chapter 17: The Poet Blogs the Layoff....................................101

Chapter 18: The Poetry of Electronic Work.............................106
Using Work to Block Creativity...109

Chapter 19: The Poetry of Workplace Restoration....................112
Poetry at Work: Airport Security...115

Chapter 20: The Poetry of Retirement....................................118

Conclusion...121

Recommended Resources 122

Notes 124

Acknowledgements 128

Foreword

By Scott Edward Anderson

On the one-year anniversary of 9/11, we held a vigil or memorial service in the office where I worked. We thought it best to set aside time to reflect, remember, and reconnect with each other.

Gathering in the conference room, we shared our memories, stories, prayers, and poems.

I read W.H. Auden's poem "September 1, 1939," and we followed it with a moment of silence. Others shared poems; told of where they were when they heard the news; someone sang a hymn, I believe; most of us cried.

It was the most powerful staff meeting I'd ever attended.

Later that day, I circulated Auden's poem by email to my colleagues at work and to a larger poetry email list I maintain for National Poetry Month.

The poem, Auden's reaction to the Nazi invasion of Poland, seemed an appropriate response to the shock we all still felt about the attack on the World Trade Center, and the massive loss of life such as we hadn't experienced on our soils since the Civil War.

Auden, writing not far from lower Manhattan, begins the poem,

I sit in one of the dives
On Fifty-second Street
Uncertain and afraid
As the clever hopes expire
Of a low dishonest decade:

Waves of anger and fear
Circulate over the bright
And darkened lands of the earth,
Obsessing our private lives;
The unmentionable odour of death
Offends the September night.

This poem was widely circulated in the aftermath of 9/11, as if the poem struck a collective chord both emotional and visceral. Great poetry is timeless.

Back in the mid-to-late '90s, I delivered a series of talks about poetry and business life to groups of corporate leaders, Rotary clubs, and small business associations. I read poems—not my own—about how it felt to fire someone, what it was like for a woman in corporate America, and why it's so hard to let go when you retire.

I loved the reactions of the businessmen in the room, especially the older men who had experienced a lot of the feelings described. Invariably, most nodded along with something that hit home; many looked skyward and blinked back tears. Poetry moved them.

Poetry at work is no longer an anomaly. David Whyte, Clare Morgan, James Autry, and others helped make it acceptable. So, too, did many individual leaders and managers who were open to letting poetry into their companies, offices, and discourse.

In *Poetry at Work*, Glynn Young argues for the poetry of work—at work, in work, and in the workplace. He finds it in the big things, such as the crisis to which he helped respond as a speechwriter for a chemical company, and in the small, everyday interactions we all experience at the office.

Long ago I received a bit of advice from an older poet who told me to go out and get a real job and write about real life. It was sage counsel and I am the better for it. I have no regrets about being a working poet rather than an academic.

I have spent my entire working life as a poet. Indeed, I was a poet even before I had my first job.

The closest I ever came to having a traditional "poetry job" was when I worked on the editorial staff at Viking Press—that and one lecture on the process of revision given at the University of Alaska, Anchorage.

I have always tried to bring my poetry to my work life and to let my work life influence my poetry. The work that lent itself best to my poetry was the fifteen years I spent with The Nature Conservancy, in part because much of my poetry is focused on the natural world and our species' relationship with it.

The Conservancy offered me opportunities for firsthand field observations, unparalleled access to the scientific knowledge of some of the world's foremost biologists, and travel to many of the Earth's last great and most spectacular places.

My time with the Conservancy provided a beautiful symbiosis between my work and my poetry. I have not since been able to reclaim that symbiosis, yet my work life still informs my poetry in other ways.

I may not find direct, poetic inspiration from my day job now, but it affects the way I work on my poetry. Rather than writing late at night after being out in the field, I now find odd, furtive moments: walking to or from the office between meetings, on the subway commute, and while waiting for elevators.

Occasionally, I'll be struck by some phrase or sentence heard on a conference call and I'll work it until finding its marrow or proving it useless. Part of it might resurface while I'm driving between cities or on an airplane or it may be lost forever.

I had a meeting a little over a year ago with a European colleague at the Grand Hyatt in New York. We were introduced by a mutual acquaintance from outside the firm for which we both work. As we met and ascended the stairs to the Lounge at New York Central, I was reminded of a poem I wrote in that bar many years ago, while working for an international publishing agency. "Drink Meeting at the Grand Hyatt Sun Garden" well-illustrated my discomfort at the time, as an artist in a business setting.

The name of the bar has changed, as has my comfort level with business life over the years.

Drink Meeting at the Grand Hyatt Sun Garden

Jazz standards fill the atrium,
black and white and one uniform shade of gray
—is this a Woody Allen film?
I'm waiting for Soandso on business,
not my business,
but the people I work for, theirs—
Any moment Woody will walk in
with Mia Farrow or Somebody,
an entourage, paparazzi.
He'll head straight for my table,
and shake my hand;
the press will want to know
who I am, and I'll no longer
be "a minor poet, not very conspicuous."

I fight the urge to bolt
out of the Sun Garden bar
and find some dark, unmonikered pub,
like those my father frequented.
I realize the discomfort he must have felt
when he'd visit the clean, well-lighted
establishments of Tokyo, or LA, or Miami
on business, not his
but the people he worked for, theirs—
This is not my world:
a foreign post for a poet
and accidental businessman.
I suspect they'd throw me out
if not for my Brooks Brothers suit
and American Express card, not mine
but the people I work for, theirs—
Soandso is late, or lost,
or has forgotten…no,
it turns out she's been waiting
in the lobby, fifteen minutes, twenty,
only just now thought
to check the bar—"Silly me…"
No Woody, no Mia, no Diane Keaton.
(But wait, isn't that Mr. Shawn by the piano?
And isn't that Donald Trump on the divan?)
Just a meeting, information shared—
perhaps, one day, we could be friends—
business transacted,
not my business,
but what has become mine—

I light a cigarette after Soandso has gone.
"Are you finished with this one, sir?"
I order another drink
and finish my poem. This
is my business.
The world is my office.

I try to bring poetry to my work life as much as possible, whether I'm giving a speech or presentation, leading trainings or writing copy for an annual report or business plan. It's not always easy to bring poetry to work, but as my friend the management consultant Cam Danielson says, poetry adds a dimension to me that others don't have—a way of paying attention to and perceiving the world that perhaps challenges or even changes the worldview of others.

In the end, we don't give ourselves enough time for poetry—at work or at home. If we did, our business life might be less stressful and more satisfying. We might find our work more rewarding. We might, as Young suggests, find the poetry at work.

—Scott Edward Anderson
　author of *Fallow Field*

Introduction

In a meeting, I discover poetry at work.

It's a weekly meeting. Same time, same people, and almost always the same agenda. We meet because meetings are mandatory to make a cross-functional network breathe. It can be mind-numbing, hearing the same weekly voices making the same weekly points, but the sameness and even the mild boredom offer the sense—or illusion—of a safe, predictable, and comfortable work environment.

Unexpectedly, I hear a submerged conversation. The same ideas, statement, voices and goals are converging to form an almost musical repetition.

Trying not to look too alarmed, I continue to listen to this music as I watch the musicians—meeting attendees—play each part. I'm discovering an underlying structure to this meeting, this music composition.

It's poetry.

I listen; I watch. Facial expressions, tone of voice, hand gestures, body language—they've all converged, orchestrated as poetry, rising from the citizens of a corporate subculture.

Then I realize something else.

Poetry has always been at work.

As I hear these sounds and rhythms and repetitions, I realize that poetry shows up not only in a weekly meeting but in many other areas of work—poetry is so embedded in the presentations we make, the spaces in which we work, and the successes and failures and challenges of work, it can't be separated from them. When we work, we express and create poetry.

I settle back in my chair, stunned that poetry has been here all along, in every job I've ever had. All I have to do is look for it.

1

How to Recognize a Poet at Work

A secretary at work stopped me outside my office. "People are worried about you," she said.

"Me?" I asked. "Why?"

"You're walking the hallways, mumbling to yourself. People are noticing."

I stared for a moment, and then I understood. "I'm writing a speech," I said. "It's a restless activity for me. I have to walk and mouth the words as I go. I have to hear them. The words have to sound right."

She nodded, relieved, if still a little worried.

I was amused, and then I realized you can always recognize the poet at work. Few of them actually wander the hallways mumbling. Poets aren't quite that odd. Usually. But you can tell who they are, even if they don't write or read poetry.

At meetings, for example, poets speak aloud what everyone else is thinking. "A dead skunk is sitting in the middle of the table," the poet in the room says, "and we're avoiding it. But it still smells."

Or the team needs to complete a project, but is depending—and waiting—on one member to finish an essential task. When the unfinished task comes out in a meeting, people look embarrassed—too embarrassed to say anything. The guilty party brazens it out in silence. The poet at the table looks around at everyone else and finally says, "Why didn't you do your assignment?"

Or a group interviews a candidate for a job using the questions supplied by Human Resources. The poet among them says, "Enough of these behavioral questions. Can't we just talk about what's important and what you need in the job?"

The poets at work make the uncomfortable observations, point out the embarrassingly obvious, cut through the thicket of workplace jargon to get straight to the point, and ask "why" about the ridiculous aspects of the organization's culture. They may never write or read a line of poetry, but they behave just like the people who do.

At best, they get classified in management reviews as "conscientious objectors." At worst, they get saddled with the most dreaded characterization of the 21st century: "not a team player." They rarely make it to senior management ranks because of their poetic tendencies. Though the culture usually wouldn't know to label these people as poets, it nonetheless recognizes a poet and will tend to respond like white blood cells fighting an infection. It stops short of eliminating the poets, however, because the organizational culture knows, deep down, that its poets are needed. Without their blunt talk stating the embarrassingly obvious— without these poets challenging the status quo—a culture has no ability to change, evolve, and grow.

Years ago, a story was told about a brilliant researcher who made it into senior management ranks. His brilliance included challenging the status quo in unorthodox ways. For example, he said he thought better while sitting in bed, so instead of a desk in his executive office, he situated a big four-poster bed right in the middle of the room. He'd make surprise visits to the research labs, bringing along a trumpet to play because he believed they were too quiet.

He didn't last long. Neither did the organization's research function. What followed were years of restructurings, eliminations, sell-offs, and downsizings.

No word on what happened to the bed.

It's right there on the table,
a piece of skunky road kill,
and we go to great lengths
not to talk about it,
not to acknowledge it,
to act in spite of it,
to plan and decide
pretending it's not there.
But it is, isn't it, safely
ignored until the poet
wanders in, mumbling.

Poetic Exercise: Think back to three different work experiences. They can be your first job, the work-study job you juggled with a crazy class schedule in college, or even what you're doing now. Did any of them include a coworker or boss who might have been the poet? How did you know? ("He acted weird" is not a sufficient answer.)

Poet Focus: William Carlos Williams

Wendell Berry's *The Poetry of William Carlos Williams of Rutherford,* a collection of essays and reflections, focuses on a theme in the life of "the poet of Rutherford" near to Berry's own heart. That theme is *place,* or what Berry refers to as "local adaptation," and he explicitly says that his purpose in writing the book was to examine "Williams' lifelong effort to come to terms with, to imagine, and to be of use to his native and chosen place."

It's tempting to think of poets as "poets," or writers, before we think of them as people with lives where they excelled at things other than poetry. Williams was known as a doctor (specifically, a pediatrician) before he became known as poet. His place: Rutherford, New Jersey, where he was "of use to his native and chosen place" as a doctor before his poetry helped put Rutherford on the map.

The Poetry Foundation's biography of Williams recognizes the importance of his medical career to his poetry: "A doctor for more than forty years serving the New Jersey town of Rutherford, he relied on his patients, the America around him, and his own ebullient imagination to create a distinctively American verse."

Williams wrote more than poetry—including essays, articles, and a collection of short stories about the practice of medicine published in a volume called *The Doctor Stories*. While that book obviously centers on his profession, you can't read his poetry for long before you notice allusions to medicine, hospitals and doctors. His famous prose/verse work *Spring and All* (1923) includes direct references:

By the road to the contagious hospital
under the surge of blue
mottled clouds driven from the
northeast – a cold wind. Beyond, the
waste of broad muddy fields
brown with dried weeds, standing and fallen

patches of standing water
the scattering of tall trees

All along the road the reddish
purplish, forked, upstanding, twiggy
stuff of bushes and small trees
with dead brown leaves under them
leafless vines –

Lifeless in appearance, sluggish
dazed spring approaches…

Even without the direct references, his poems benefit from his
training and immersion in medicine: His poems are written with
a keen, observing eye—the eye of a doctor, a physician who can't
always rely on what his patients tell him or what he can directly
observe, because he knows so much may be hidden and
unknown.

On a wall at St. Mary's Hospital in Rutherford, a plaque has
been placed recognizing Williams for both his poetry and his
practice of medicine. It reads:

"We walk the wards where Williams walked"
1883-1963
William Carlos Williams MD
Poet Physician
Member of This Medical Staff
1924-1963

And then it concludes with a quote by the poet physician: "The poem springs from the half spoken words of the patient."

The poetry of William Carlos Williams cannot really be separated from his work as a physician. I suspect his work as a physician cannot be separated from his poetry, either. Both are facets of the same person, a whole person—a man who wrote poetry with a doctor's eye and practiced medicine with the compassion of a poet.

2

The Poetry of the Interview

I was part of an interview team talking individually with four candidates for a communication research job. Human Resources had provided us with a set of "behavioral interview" questions, which meant we would be asking things like "What's the biggest failure you've ever experienced?" and "Where do you see yourself in ten years?" Those are two of the better questions. Behavioral interviews have reigned supreme in organizational employment for some time. They haven't improved with age and experience, but you deal with them.

The interview team met, sorted through the questions, decided who would ask each one, and determined what we really needed to know about the candidates to discern how they well they would fit the position. For this job, we knew we needed someone willing to be blunt, able to resist pressure, and even though the work seemed mundane, we needed a creative person who could energize this role.

We were talking with our fourth and final candidate. We had dutifully followed the HR guidelines, but we went slightly off script to get at the considerations we were particularly concerned with. I had asked one additional question of the previous three candidates and now asked the fourth.

"What do you think of our website?"

The first three had gushed about how wonderful it was. They knew I was the one whose team was responsible for it.

The fourth said it was rather boring and uninteresting.

We had found the poet in the group, the one who would not let desire for a job stand in the way of professional honesty.

Guess which candidate we hired?

Whole sections of libraries and myriad consulting firms have been built around the job interview, with those predictable "behavioral interview questions" serving as the current interview canon. Rather than ask people how they overcame a career setback, I'd prefer to ask them who their favorite poet or writer is.

This can work in reverse, too, when you're the job candidate. Once, a CEO interviewing me for a speechwriting job asked if I had any additional questions, and I asked him what he read outside of work. The question wasn't an idle one; I had worked for a CEO who read John Updike's novels and one whose idea of extracurricular reading was the *Harvard Business Review*. That question provided insight into their minds and hearts.

This particular CEO was initially surprised, and then, rather sheepishly, answered "murder mysteries and police procedurals." He saw my eyes light up, and we talked for the next thirty minutes about favorite authors and favorite mysteries. (And, yes, I got the job.)

Asking a question like that instead of those behaviorally correct questions we use today might turn up something unexpected. You might learn that a candidate (or potential boss) doesn't like or read poetry, for example. While that doesn't disqualify, it might speak volumes about how a candidate thinks.

An interviewer can insert the poetry question directly into the interaction, but even if he can't probe the poetic interests of a candidate, he can certainly participate in the inherent poetry of job interviews. For both the interviewer and the candidate, these conversations contain drama, anxiety, tension, hope, fear, uncertainty—emotions and realities that make for great poetry. Plus, the interplay between the two people contains its own inner poetry as one expresses organizational need and the other, individual desire. Then each switches to promise benefits to the other.

In an interview, questions and answers are both imagined and practiced before the actual event. Both interviewers and candidates do this, searching for the right words that will crystallize thoughts and express ideas in exactly the right way. Sound something like poetry?

Interviews, like poetry, are ultimately about ideas, even though they are ostensibly about people. Behind the people in an interview are ideas about careers, employment, the future, and organizational goals and objectives. Behind a poem is experience, personal and group history, philosophy, how one understands the world, and even hope for a different or changed future.

Consider an interview to be the beginning of a poem. Interviewers and candidates come together, and relationships are born, if only briefly. Something new occurs. The job interview, like a poem, can be mundane and perfunctory, but it can also be inspirational.

> Tell me a poem, a story
> of a favored poet or poem,
> one who changed your life,
> your mind, opened up
> possibilities, or made you
> feel secure as your anchors,
> your moorings, were removed.

Speak to me of your need;
describe the expectations
(are they great ones?), explain
how we soar together, toward
the sun, if not the moon,
tell me how I become

part of your larger self.

Poetic Exercise: Imagine you're being interviewed for a job. You're being asked the standard questions, and you've read enough articles and books on the subject of interviews to handle every one of them. Then the interviewer asks, "Who's your favorite poet?"

After recovering from the surprise, keeping your face impassive while you think of a response that won't ruin your prospects for the job, you answer. So here's the exercise:

If your answer is Walt Whitman, what does that tell the interviewer about you?

What would "Emily Dickinson" suggest?

Try "Wallace Stevens" or "Nikki Giovanni." Where does that lead the interviewer?

Or what if you opt for "I don't have a favorite poet; I don't read poetry"?

Poet Focus: Wallace Stevens

I generally had fine English teachers in high school and college, teachers who emphasized poetry as much as they did other literary forms. From the *Iliad* through *Beowulf* and Chaucer, and then on to romantics, Victorians and moderns, I probably read as much poetry as I did anything else.

And then, for close to a decade, I read little, if any, focusing on career, family, and "getting established." I read fiction when I could find time.

That changed when I became part of a company's speechwriting team. No one else on the team read poetry (all history majors), but a friend kept pressing on me the need to read poetry if I was really serious about being a speechwriter. He gave me copies of the collected poems of three great modernist poets: T. S. Eliot, Dylan Thomas and Wallace Stevens. It didn't take much convincing; I could easily see that poetry and speeches— truly fine speeches—have much in common in terms of form, flow, cadence, voice, rhythm and how they sound to the ear. Differences exist, to be sure, but I readily saw that I could learn much about speechwriting from poetry.

I was familiar with Eliot and Thomas from my formal education years. Wallace Stevens (1879 – 1955) was something of a revelation. A businessman with the heart of a poet. A corporate attorney, who turned down academic offers from Ivy League universities to stay with the Hartford Insurance Company.

While he likely stayed in business for financial reasons, I'm confident Stevens also found inspiration in his corporate work and the drama it provided in human conflict, success and failure, victory and defeat, blood and sweat and even tears. Plans go awry. Events, trends and people are misjudged. Mistakes are made. Success can often be the result of serendipity rather than the purposeful execution of programs.

This is the stuff of poetry. And while Wallace Stevens may

not have written poems overtly about corporations and the insurance business, in a sense he really did.

Poets in business hear things others can miss. Every workplace conversation has an interior and overt stream, and it's usually the poet who hears the interior dialogues before others do, because they are shaped by words and phrases originating in hopes, dreams and fears.

While it's likely not the origin of this poem, imagine a woman who discovers that her recently deceased husband had cancelled his insurance policy, or named someone else the beneficiary.

Another Weeping Woman
By Wallace Stevens

Pour the unhappiness out
From your too bitter heart,
Which grieving will not sweeten.

Poison grows in this dark.
It is in the water of tears
Its black blooms rise.

The magnificent cause of being,
The imagination, the one reality
In this imagined world

Leaves you
With him for whom no phantasy moves,
And you are pierced by a death.

3

The Poetry of the Workspace

My office is decent; I have no complaints. It is ten-foot square with enough room to accommodate a narrow coat closet, a credenza with file drawers, a desk, two visitor chairs, and a four-shelf bookcase. And it has a window. A closed-door office with a window is a big deal and immediately communicates a certain work grade level, a certain status. It would communicate even more status if I didn't have, pushed against the one wall free of furniture, boxes with stuff piled on top to be sorted for the corporate archives.

I usually keep the shade closed. When I first moved into the space, the window overlooked the building's designated smoking area. Clouds of smoke hovered outside the window and obscured the view. I had to stand and then look at an angle to get a better view. Later the smoking area was confined to a covered patio-like area on the other side of the building, but I still must stand up and then turn to catch a glimpse of the tall oak tree in the courtyard, the grassy slope extending down and away from the building, or the stark outline of the research center which forms my visual horizon.

Workspace is important, and not because of status implications. It's the physical area where a person may spend years being creative, productive, and (to embrace that current buzz phrase) adding value. To create and "optimize" workspace, large organizations tend to follow whatever management theory is in vogue at the moment, building or remodeling to suit that theory.

In the 1940s and 1950s, big open spaces were all the rage, especially in functions like finance and accounting. The '60s and '70s brought a lot of enclosed offices—my first job at a large corporation in Houston found me in an 8×12 office which contained the department's large storage closet; whatever cachet came with the office was lost in the steady parade of people walking through it to get to the closet. In the '80s and '90s, cubicle farms could be found all over when collaboration and teams became the rule. My current workplace's mix of cubicle farms and regular offices suggests that collaboration is still important but so are individual contributions, and that this is a hierarchy after all.

A workspace contains a certain rhythm and cadence and language and flow and structure and, well, poetry, that characterizes these places where work gets done. The utilitarian cubicle, for example, might be compared to the minimalist, spare structure of the haiku. The two best speeches I ever wrote were both composed in a cubicle—the spare, simple language of the texts mirrored the sparseness of that workspace. A conference room, by comparison, is a kind of villanelle, where certain things (or lines) get endlessly repeated.

Language is spoken and written in workspaces. Ideas are communicated—sometimes well, sometimes not. Conflicts and problems arise to be resolved, or are ignored and left to fester. People are encouraged, reprimanded, lauded and belittled; people create and perform; people manage and survive and flourish and wither.

Poetry happens in workspaces because life happens in workspaces. It may the formal language of the U. S. Supreme Court, the screaming of the commodity exchanges in Chicago, the quiet tension of a difficult corporate board meeting, or the reality of trying to maintain order in an inner city school. It may be the jangle of the radio dispatcher enclosed in a police car, the impassioned sermon from the minister in church, or the roar of the crowd at the World Series. It may be the last words breathed in the hospice bed.

Whether the space is the Oval Office, a classroom, a home, the cab of a truck or taxi, a warehouse, an assembly line, a shop or a store, an offshore oil rig, a hair salon, or an office cubicle, emotion happens there. Life happens there. And the dramas and comedies and occasional tragedies that unfold there matter.

This is all poetry. And it matters.

Words swirl around my space,
seeking a home, a purpose,
commanding they be noticed
or translated into bits
and pixels to ricochet
upon screens and minds and hopes.
Images on my walls stare
in framed, silent witness.

Poetic Exercise: Take a hard look at the space you work in. Consider its physical size, the sounds and the smells, the amount of natural light versus light fixtures. What is the most obvious thing about it? Ask yourself what makes this particular space unique, and what makes it similar to other workspaces near yours. Write down some of the really good things you've accomplished in your workspace.

No matter how simple and plain or complex and luxurious, your workspace contains poetry. Can you find it? Can you write a short poem about it?

Poet Focus: Dana Gioia

Dana Gioia is a poet, essayist, former chairman of the National Endowment for the Arts—and a former vice president of marketing for General Foods (now part of Kraft). In 1991, while he was still helping sell Jell-O®, he wrote an article for *The Atlantic* entitled "Can Poetry Matter," which caused something of an uproar in the poetry world.

Gioia argued that poetry had been captured by academia and had become disconnected from its reading public. Poetry was in danger of becoming irrelevant to anyone except poets, who were increasingly the people who taught poetry.

Yes, he was a published poet, but he was also a business executive—a business executive who could write a well-argued essay about literary culture.

The outrage came from academia. But something quite different came from the reading public—especially those who read poetry, serious fiction, criticism and essays, and who live and work outside universities. They agreed with Gioia, and they, too, said poetry was no longer important to either American culture or American literary culture.

Gioia's argument was not new; in his essay, he pointed out that Edmund Wilson had expressed similar sentiments in the 1930s and Joseph Epstein in the 1980s. What was new was his direct frontal attack on the poetry establishment that spilled over into the public consciousness. And he pointed to the proliferation of poetry journals, readings and events that were happening outside of "established" poetry.

Ten years later, in a revised collection of essays, he reiterated the point he made in 1991 and pointed to the Internet as an additional phenomenon underscoring the divide between the academy and the reading public, who were taking poetry online. (And in the decade since, the rise of YouTube, Facebook, Twitter and other social media have done even more to make poetry "public.")

Gioia didn't simply complain about the state of poetry; he suggested six actions poets could take to move poetry out of academic circles and into the minds of the reading public—the audience that had been largely abandoned:

1. At public readings, poets should read other poets' work in addition to their own.

2. Poetry readings should mix poetry with the other arts, like music.

3. Poets should write prose about poetry more often, and more candidly.

4. Poets assembling anthologies should include only the poems they admire, not the poems that teachers might require in the classroom.

5. Poetry teachers should spend less time on analysis and more on performance.

6. And radio should be used to expand the reach of poetry.

As poetry becomes more prominent in the context of literary life, and more broadly in the context of everyday life, poetry can naturally reach into companies and organizations, impacting people in their work. More poetry at work? That's a very good thing.

4

The Poetry of the Commute

With the exception of a few months in 2000 when I worked from home, my career has included the daily bookends of a commute—as short as a mile when I drove to my office in the town center of our St. Louis suburb, and as long as seventeen miles when my wife and I lived in Houston and traveled from a northwest suburb to our jobs downtown.

A commute of a mile is a short ode: Joyce Kilmer talking about a tree, over and done with before you realize it, your car's engine barely warmed up. For my one-mile commute in our suburb, I drove almost literally through a Joyce Kilmer poem thanks to the tree-lined streets leading to our "downtown," whose two-story historic buildings, small train station and farmer's market seemed like a Wendell Berry small town—complete with Jayber Crow's barber shop.

Our commute of seventeen miles into downtown Houston was radically different, like driving Homer's *Odyssey* twice a day, complete with Medusa, the Cyclops, and—once—a martial dispute that ended as a shoot-out on the freeway witnessed by Houstonian commuters apathetic toward this domestic tragedy, outraged instead at how badly traffic was messed up as a result. No tree-lined streets there; instead, we traveled seventeen miles of concrete freeway, bumper-to-bumper for miles at a time. And, like *The Odyssey,* we spent an enormous amount of usually wasted time and effort trying to find a way—any way—home.

For our first six years in St. Louis, my commute was about a mile-and-a-half, and then we moved to our current home some six miles from my office. Except for our highway "belt" around the city, most commuters in St. Louis move east and west, I commute north and south. Traveling north to work on a boulevard, I sometimes encounter congestion at intersections and stoplights, but the trip usually takes only about fifteen minutes. The route cuts through several extended wooded suburbs. For my southward commute home, I take a parallel road—a two-lane journey that cuts through one of the wealthiest parts of St. Louis, and, indeed, the entire state of Missouri. I know now why they call wealthy parts of cities "leafy." Driving in both directions is driving through Tennyson, Kipling, and Longfellow, the sense of a place for everything and everything in its place, an orderly world of manicured lawns and Edith Wharton sensibilities.

Why take different ways in the morning and evening? In the morning, the four-lane boulevard misses all the traffic associated with two fairly large high schools on the two-lane road. In the evening, the schools have usually let out, and a lot of traffic is flowing on the four-lane boulevard. Think of it as tackling the complexities of T. S. Eliot in the morning, and choosing the relative simplicity of Emily Dickinson in the evening.

When I worked for St. Louis Public Schools from 2003 to 2004, I commuted sixteen miles to downtown via the main east-west interstate highway. While nothing like that Odyssey we experienced in Houston, congestion still ruled and driving the highway meant a journey through a concrete canyon.

Becoming aware of the poetry I'm finding at work, I've discovered recently that poetry extends to the oh-so-prosaic commute that we travel hundreds or thousands of times without paying much attention to the local geography. I look for it in that first mile of car dealerships, grocery stores and fast food restaurants, and then I turn to the right and travel two miles through what's known as the region's "horse country"—the village of Huntleigh, population 780 and about the same number of horses, the suburb of landed estates that at one time marked the far western developed edge of the region.

Huntleigh becomes Frontenac, a larger suburb with smaller lot sizes but still a lot of wealth. And then Frontenac gives way to Creve Coeur, yet another wealthy suburb. These names suggest medieval chivalry, aristocratic fox hunts, and poetry of the 18th century—formal, upper-class, and proper—while disguising smoldering emotions behind the names. I think of King Arthur's crève-coeur at the betrayal of Lancelot and Guinevere.

Finally I reach the campus where I work, some 800 acres of parking lots, office buildings and large stretches of woods. The Age of Reason dominates here, lettered buildings in a campus-like setting, science and technology as developed as anything you'd find in Silicon Valley. Yet the woods (and the trails through the woods) lead me right into the Romantics. At several points the woods completely envelop the trails, and I can imagine myself in a national forest.

Driving, of course, isn't the only kind of commute where poetry can be found.

Poetry of the Underground

On a recent vacation in London, my wife and I rode the District line tube from St. James's Park to Embankment station.

We changed trains for the Northern line, on our way to Leicester Square and a short walk to a restaurant in Soho, where we were meeting a friend for lunch.

We avoided rush hour and easily found seats. My eyes naturally went to the Tube map above the windows across from us to count how many stations before we had to exit. Only the Westminster remained until Embankment. And then I saw, right next to the map, the printed text of a poem: "Buses on the Strand," by R. P. Lister:

> The Strand is beautiful with buses,
> Fat and majestical in form,
> Red like tomatoes in their trusses
> In August, when the sun is warm…

Poems on the Underground, a project of Transport for London, makes the daily commute on the Tube less, well, uneventful, by exposing more people to poetry. The full texts of poems are posted alongside ads, instructional notices, and the Tube map.

The program began in 1986, the brainchild of an American, Judith Chernaik. Poems are displayed on about 3,000 spaces on the Underground trains. The London Transport Museum has been publishing collections of the poems for several years.

Poems on the Underground isn't the oldest such program. In 1984, *Streetfare Journal* began producing posters combining art and literature for buses in several U. S. cities.

Both Poems on the Underground and *Streetfare Journal* inspired the Poetry in Motion program. In 1992, the Metropolitan Transit Authority, partnering with the Poetry Society of America, placed poems on public transportation to reach some seven million commuters. One of the first poems displayed was—surprise—Walt Whitman's "Crossing Brooklyn Ferry."

Poetic Exercise: Write down your path to and from work. It doesn't matter if your commute is by car, public transportation, foot or bicycle. Whether it's a commute of 100 miles or the distance from the kitchen to your home office, write down the details of what you see. If you commute by wheels (car, bus, motorcycle, bicycle, skateboard), note the buildings, scenes and sights you pass. Or the billboards and road signs (I sometimes play a game of trying to say the words on a street sign backwards—can tell what this is: "p mar n rut u"?).

Then ask yourself, is there poetry here? Could I write a poem using the names of the streets I pass? Could I write about the three grocery stories, one large hotel and shopping center I pass? What about the driver who's talking on his cell phone? (I have a poem for those drivers—one of the circles of Dante's *Inferno*.)

Poet Focus: Carl Sandburg

Carl Sandburg's *Chicago Poems* was published in 1916, when he was 34 years old. "Chicago," the poem that helped establish his reputation, was published in *Poetry* magazine two years before that. (It contains the line Chicagoans love: "City of the Big Shoulders.")

As I read those poems collected with "Chicago" and the others grouped under the headings of "Fogs and Fires," "Shadows," and "Other Days," the words and themes and ideas seemed familiar.

Sandburg's *Chicago Poems* is of the same root as Upton Sinclair's novel *The Jungle*. Sinclair told the story of the plight of immigrants at the turn of the 20th century and how employers, landlords and shopkeepers exploited them. The novel caused quite a stir when it was published, but not for reasons Sinclair had hoped. Readers focused on the descriptions of the meat-packing industry, and national outrage led to the passage of the Pure Food and Drug Act, which established the Food & Drug Administration. Everyone forgot about the immigrants.

In *Chicago Poems*, Sandburg writes about the immigrants and laborers who helped turn Chicago into the economic power-house it became. And many of the poems clearly have a Sinclair kind of feel to them. Take "Onion Days," for example:

Mrs. Gabrielle Giovannitti comes along Peoria Street every
    morning at nine o'clock
With kindling wood piled on top of her head, her eyes
    looking straight ahead to find the way for her old feet.
Her daughter-in-law, Mrs. Pietro Giovannitti, whose husband
    was killed in a tunnel explosion through the negligence
    of a fellow-servant,
Works ten hours a day, sometimes twelve, picking onions for
    Jasper on the Bowmanville road.

Jasper, as it turns out, sits in his Episcopal church service, enjoys the chanting of the Nicene Creed, and plans how to advertise the onion-picking jobs so he can attract even more applicants and drive wages down.

The Sandburg poems evoke the same kind of thoughts and feelings as paintings by Edward Hopper. I've written three poems about Hopper paintings, and reading these Sandburg poems brought those paintings to mind. Chronologically, Sinclair, Sandburg and Hopper were of overlapping generations. Sinclair and Sandburg also had a strong Chicago connection. And one of Hopper's most famous paintings, "Nighthawks," hangs in the The Art Institute of Chicago. Finding the threads that tied these three together pointed to the way culture can be changed by the work of artist and poet.

Sandburg's poems are of a place and period—even awkwardly of a time period, as some of them include language and ethnic nicknames that would be deemed politically incorrect today. But they made connections for me to art, literature and history, reminding me that poetry can be expressed in a way that transcends time and place, touching on universal themes while simultaneously remaining rooted in a particular time, inviting us back to an era that is otherwise lost to us all.

5

The Poetry of the Boss

For decades, stretching back at least to the 1920s when "management" began to emerge as a "science," leadership has been a serious business subject to study, pursue, obtain a degree in, and apply in the workplace. (Peter Drucker began writing on the subject in the late 1930s.)

What workplace leadership should and shouldn't do has changed over the years, much as workplace structures have changed and are still changing. Corporations, for example, modeled management after the command-and-control image of the military, leading to the origin of "staff" functions we're so familiar with today. The military metaphor fit a mass-production, hierarchal, management-style economy.

Command-and-control management didn't inspire much poetry, but it did give birth to a considerable number of novels, like Sloan Wilson's *The Man in the Gray Flannel Suit* (1955), *The Embezzler* by Louis Auchincloss (1966), and Charles Bukowski's *Post Office* (1971).

The management metaphor began to change in the 1960s and 1970s. The famous "plastics" scene in the 1967 film *The Graduate* signaled a shift, with the business executive telling the young Dustin Hoffman to pursue a career in plastics, and his words making no sense to Hoffman whatsoever. The command-and-control boss knew all the answers and all the questions, too. This paternalistic system began to fall apart in the 1980s when the promise of orderly and lifetime employment began dissolving in waves of restructurings and downsizings.

This conflict and human drama could have easily been the subject of poetry, but it largely wasn't—perhaps a result of poetry being firmly ensconced within academia.

Instead of poetry, management consulting firms gave us a wave of "best practices." One of the bibles of this wave, *In Search of Excellence* by Thomas J. Peters and Robert H. Waterman, remained a go-to resource for years until people began to notice that the companies singled out for excellence didn't remain successful.

The "best practices" era was a hard time to be a boss. So much was changing; so much conventional wisdom was being thrown out. In this period, poet David Whyte published *The Heart Aroused: Poetry and the Preservation of the Soul in Corporate America*. His was one of the first works answering the questions of the workplace—the big questions—directly by poetry. His book arrived after a decade of tumultuous change in corporate America and the corporate world globally—downsizings, restructurings, mergers, and structural experiments were grinding out ever more efficient ways to do work, or ways that claimed to be more efficient.

The corporate soul was suffering, and David Whyte had an answer—poetry. "The poet needs the practicalities of making a living to test and temper the lyricism of insight and observation," Whyte said. "The corporation needs the poet's insight and powers of attention in order to weave the inner world of soul and creativity with the outer world of form and matter."

Whyte's words spoke straight to my heart and affirmed my role as a poet in the workplace. I had been a CEO's speechwriter.

I had been reading poetry for more than fifteen years to write better speeches. I was also caught up in the transformation of the workplace by the electronic communications revolution and a huge influx of new thinking about corporations, their organizational structures, and whether they would function best as machines or networks.

I faced the first rush of the email avalanche and the advent of the website—a time when staff functions were turned upside down in the name of rationality and efficiency while candy was distributed at meetings and spirit teams went around headquarters singing to people. Senior executives were spinning off businesses and following the instructions of consultants in meetings while playing with LEGO blocks to release their inner child.

This was touchy-feely "Kumbaya" around the campfire existing next to marketplace ruthlessness. These were not two sides of the same coin. They were completely different coins, existing simultaneously, representing radically-polarized visions of the future. Neither was sustainable.

"Our lack of soul is our refusal to open to a full experience in the world," Whyte said. "Work, paradoxically, does not ask enough of us, yet exhausts the narrow parts of us we do bring to its door." In the book, Whyte used Beowulf; poems by Robert Frost, Pablo Neruda, and T. S. Eliot; the Irish folk tale of "Fionn and the Salmon of Knowledge"; and the poetry of Coleridge to make his points about the individual soul in corporate America, the soul being "the indefinable essence of a person's spirit and being."

It is in the soul—that place in the depths of our existence—where storms often rage and chaos is more the norm than the exception. We don't just bring our skills, talents, experience and physical bodies to the workplace; we also bring our souls, as much as systems management tries to deny and fight it.

I was a boss, struggling with how to lead people as organizational chaos unleashed all around us. Poetry and *The Heart Aroused* helped me make sense of what was happening. The result was not a "happy medium" or compromise. Instead, I ended up rejecting both, seeing them for the shams they were, these extremes of institutionalized hippiedom and the killing machine of rationalized efficiency. Instead, I found understanding of what was happening and, eventually, a path forward both for myself and for the people I was leading.

The network is developing as one possible new model—more than one expert has noted that we tend to organize our workplaces along the lines of the prevailing technology. Social media and the Internet have changed everything yet again. Senior executives and mid-level bosses are second-guessed like never before. Executives giving bad speeches are live-tweeted. Missteps and failures (and embarrassments) live forever on the web. And yet, facets of the command-and-control structure are still with us; not every decision can be made by a team.

So what's a boss to do? How does he or she manage in a complex, unsettled, fluid workplace? Muddle through, ignore reality, or, as Whyte suggests, read *Beowulf*?

It's not easy.

> Stares at the corner where
> two glass walls meet, almost
> the exact point where the sun
> sets, caught in the rise
> of his people asking, probing

how and more and the descent
of this own boss seeking cuts.
He chooses the way
he's been taught, looking
upward, knowing there's little
reward in the daily, where
life is.

Poetic Exercise: Consider your boss. Or perhaps, more safely, consider a previous boss—your very first boss from your first job in high school, your boss at an internship, or your first boss after graduating from college. Whether the experience was good or bad, consider that boss through a poetic lens. In other words, write about that boss in a poem, using the form of poetry to explain, celebrate, understand, or even forgive.

What Poetry Brings to Business

In 2010, Clare Morgan, director of the graduate writing center at the University of Oxford, published *What Poetry Brings to Business*, coauthored with Kirsten Lange and Ted Buswick of the Boston Consulting Group. She references literary works—some well known like Robert Frost's "Stopping by Woods on a Snowy Evening" and some not so well known—to approach her subject, merging academic and business styles, referencing terminology and concepts familiar to the corporate ear such as "business processes" and case studies.

And she explores what poetry can bring to business from about every perspective imaginable, including how poetry can help you think beyond facts; how poetry and business share major themes; how poetry can apply to business decision making; how poetry can increase business creativity; and how poetry applies to business values, like corporate social responsibility. She packages and explains concepts and practices of poetry for business consumption using case studies, practical exercises, team projects, and examples of her own seminars for businesses and business groups. Morgan says:

> Precision is vital to a poet, precision of language, of image, of nuance, of tone. But the indirection poetry deals in has to do with the rejection of "facts" as the basis of its utterance. A poet isn't trying to tell you something. He isn't trying to tell you anything. The poet is taking you on a journey of exploration, and where you arrive in the end, and the nature of the journey, will be different for each person. There are no maps, no certainties.

Business leans on maps and certainties. The modern corporation was created in part to reduce uncertainty (and risk). Yet businesses have been learning for the past 30 years that, just as Morgan observes in poetry, there are no certainties, and precious few maps. As this lesson sinks in, the business world would do well to listen to Morgan's claim that poetry might suggest ways forward, or at least help us think while going forward.

Morgan sees poetry as something that exists outside of business, or really any kind of organizational life—an entity separate from the day-to-day reality of business and work that can be brought in to advise and shed light. She would apply poetry directly to how business is done, to help offer new perspectives in the form of poetic consultation.

I take it a step further than Morgan. Rather than seeing poets as outsiders speaking into the corporate world, I believe that poetry already exists within business and work. Though they may be largely ignored and unrecognized, I've seen poets and poetry within the business world—insiders, if you will, who are vital to the ongoing operation and success of what we call work. They just need to be given the freedom to do what they do best: help navigate uncharted territory and speak with poetic precision to lead the way.

6

The Poetry of Vision Statements

In the last 25 years or so, vision statements have grown to become a staple of organizational life. Companies, universities, hospitals, government agencies, even individuals have vision statements. They also routinely confuse them with mission statements.

A vision statement, in its purest form, describes what an organization aspires to be. A mission statement is how the organization intends to achieve that vision. The shorthand version: what we want to be, and what we're doing to get there.

I've read hundreds of vision statements over the years, and the best usually originate in the mind of a single individual— someone we might call an organizational poet. You can read a vision statement and know immediately whether an individual produced it, perhaps with input from a few others, or whether a committee or series of committees churned it out. An individually-written statement usually strives for one idea; the committee-composed version (assisted by the Legal Department) tries to include everything to make sure nothing (and no department) is omitted.

When done well, both vision statements and mission statements can read like a fine, moving poem.

In my career, I've written two corporate vision statements. The first one was accidental. I wrote a speech for the CEO, and the conclusion contained a series of statements that reached for something far beyond the company's current performance. It stuck, almost overnight. The second one, also part of a speech, was intentionally designed to be a vision statement. A year later, a committee got involved and rewrote part of it. That company still uses it more than a decade later and you can readily identify the speechwriter portion from the committee section.

Here are examples of vision statements (none of which I wrote). Which ones do you find truly inspirational?

Johnson & Johnson • *Vision statement:* Caring for the world, one person at a time. *Mission statement:* We embrace research and science—bringing innovative ideas, products and services to advance the health and well-being of people. Employees of the Johnson & Johnson Family of Companies work with partners in health care to touch the lives of over a billion people every day, throughout the world. (J&J also has a credo of its four responsibilities to customers, employees, communities and stockholders.)

Nike • *Vision statement (they call it their "Mission"):* To Bring Inspiration and Innovation to Every Athlete in the World.

Google • *Vision statement (which is also a kind of mission statement):* Google's mission is to organize the world's information and make it universally accessible and useful. (For an enjoyable read, look up Google's "Ten Things We Know to Be True.")

Robert Mondavi Winery • *Vision statement:* Robert Mondavi Winery strives to create wines that stand in the company of the world's finest.

State Farm Insurance • *Vision statement (another "Mission")*: State Farm's mission is to help people manage the risks of everyday life, recover from the unexpected, and realize their dreams.

The U.S. Department of Defense • *Vision statement:* The mission of the Department of Defense is to provide the military forces needed to deter war and to protect the security of our country.

Harvard University • *Vision statement:* Harvard University is devoted to excellence in teaching, learning, and research, and to developing leaders in many disciplines who make a difference globally.

St. Louis Public Schools • *Vision statement:* St. Louis Public Schools is the district of choice for families in the St. Louis region that provides a world-class education and is nationally recognized as a leader in student achievement and teacher quality. *Mission statement:* We will provide a quality education for all students and enable them to realize their full intellectual potential.

As a group, the government units (DOD, St. Louis Public Schools) are the most committee-like. Harvard's falls flat. The winery's needs some work. Google's comes off business-like, but it's not bad. Johnson & Johnson's reads the simplest—always a good thing for vision statements. Nike's inspires. I like State Farm's the best, likely because the speechwriter-poet in me likes the use of the triad. It's also helpful in the online world to have a vision statement that can be contained within a 140-character tweet on Twitter. Even better, keep it to 120 characters, leaving room for others to retweet it easily.

Of course, vision statements are not limited to organizations. People can also compose their own personal vision statements. I've done that informally. My personal vision statements have changed over the years, because I've learned that things like careers and success are less important than other things—things like people, beauty, and grandchildren.

My current vision: "To do good work each day. To comfort where I find hurt. To encourage where I find fear. To defend where I find wrong. To serve where I find need. To supply where I find want. And to see the combination of all as the greatest of these."

A vision statement, whether personal or organizational, is aspirational. It doesn't necessarily have to be true at this moment, or completely true. But it must contain at least the germ of truth so as to be believable and credible, especially to the individual or organization creating it. And, like poetry, the reader or listener finds himself nodding. "Yes, this is who we are...this is who we should be."

Poetic Exercise: How would you rewrite one of those vision statements above? Could you write it poetically and yet still make it a statement for an organization's vision?

Or consider writing a personal vision statement. Could you write one in poetic form? How would writing a personal vision statement in poetic form change what you're trying to say?

Poet Focus: Ted Kooser

Ted Kooser began his working career as a high school English teacher in 1962. He's currently the Presidential Professor of English at the University of Nebraska-Lincoln, where he's taught since 2000. He won a Pulitzer Prize for poetry and was named U.S. Poet Laureate in 2004.

Between 1963 and 1999, Kooser wrote and published poetry, but all those years he was also something else: Ted Kooser, insurance company executive.

Born in Ames, Iowa, in 1939, Kooser graduated from Iowa State University in 1962, and first worked in a high school. He then enrolled in a graduate writing program at the University of Nebraska. The Poetry Foundation states he "essentially flunked out a year later." He had to eat, so he went to work for an insurance company in Lincoln in 1964 as an underwriter and worked in the insurance industry until 1999. At the end of his insurance career, he was a vice president of public relations for the Lincoln Benefit Life Company, now part of Allstate.

The comparison to Wallace Stevens is irresistible. Stevens worked for an insurance company his entire career, even turning down an offer of a teaching position at an Ivy League University arranged by friends and admirers. Kooser has heard the comparison and said the difference was Stevens, as a corporate attorney, had more time to write poetry on the job.

The University of Nebraska Press published his first book of poetry, *Official Entry Blank*, in 1969 ("essentially flunking out" seems not to have mattered to the publisher). Some fifteen additional volumes followed, distributed by a wide array of publishers. In addition to a Pulitzer Prize and the U. S. Poet Laureate honors, Kooser has also received a Pushcart Prize, the Stanley Kunitz Prize, a Nebraska Book Award, and two fellowships from the National Endowment for the Arts, among many other recognitions.

He's been called "the poet of the Great Plains," but his lean, spare poetry surpasses a regional designation, drawing pictures of people and life familiar to most of us. Though rooted in the region, its appeal—and what it speaks to—is universal.

His poetry evokes images of aging family members, rural and farm life, home, the wonder of natural beauty, a blind woman joyfully caught in the rain, a birthday card sent by a sick aunt, stars in a night sky, a porch swing—the simple things of everyday life, things too easy to overlook and too important not to.

Most of Kooser's poetry was published during his insurance career. He did not see the two lines of work—insurance and poetry—in opposition to each other. Like Wallace Stevens, the differences notwithstanding, Kooser composed most of his poetry outside the academy, in a perhaps surprising place: an office at an insurance company.

7

The Poetry of PowerPoint

Three years ago, I wrote a post on my personal blog that is still my single most visited post. The title: "I Hate PowerPoint."

The title should have been, "I Hate PowerPoint Presentations." PowerPoint® is just a tool; the problem lies in how we use or misuse it. And we tend to use it badly. We treat it like the canvas for Homer's *Iliad* when we should instead treat it like the backdrop for a haiku.

PowerPoint was originally created to handle charts and graphs, which it can do admirably well. The problem arises with words. We presenters like words—lots of words—and we want to use every single one of them on a PowerPoint slide.

PowerPoint experts recommend no more than six to eight words per slide. Can you recall the last time you saw a PowerPoint slide with no more than eight words on it? Can you recall the last time you *created* a PowerPoint slide with no more than eight words on it?

One time I sat through a PowerPoint presentation containing more than 60 slides. Each slide had been masterfully designed to eliminate all white space, resulting in a wildly colorful combination of charts, graphs, graphics and words.

Each slide contained an average of more than 200 words. Sixty slides.

The presenter read the words on each slide. No one understood what the presentation was about. No one remembered it later, except to reference the mind-numbing ordeal we had experienced. The speaker became something of an inside joke, and his presentation a hallmark for how not to do PowerPoint presentations.

He wrote the *Iliad*, badly, when a haiku would have sufficed.

We're instinctively aware of PowerPoint mishandling. Many of us don't even use the phrase "PowerPoint presentations." Instead, we use the rather inelegant word "deck," as in, "Do you have your deck loaded on the laptop for the presentation?"

Yet, PowerPoint handled well contains a minimalist kind of poetry, including the poetry of art: pictures, photographs, drawings, cartoons. Most TED talks include PowerPoint slides, but they don't cram them with words. The very best TED talks involve an articulate, intelligent speaker who relies on a careful composition of minimalist slides that use art, visuals, and a few relevant words to supplement the main points. The slides illustrate the speaker's message instead of serving as the speaker's script to be read aloud.

When crafting a presentation in the workplace, go minimalist. Tap into the poetry of PowerPoint, approaching it as a poet approaches a poem, showing restraint, carefully selecting only the words that convey the message simply, clearly. To the poet, each word matters. Each word is carefully selected. Each word evokes a picture, a mood, an emotion.

To create a poetic PowerPoint, select words with this same precision, envisioning the entire presentation as a single poem…not each slide as a poem. With the latter approach, you've created a unified message in an economy of words; with the former approach, the presentation ends up the complete *Norton Anthology of Poetry*. A PowerPoint presentation is not Milton's "Paradise Lost," or Tennyson's "Idylls of the King."

Think small, simple, and powerful.

Poetic Exercise: Create a PowerPoint presentation that consists of one slide. Write a poem on that slide, using no more than eight words. Read it aloud.

Or take a PowerPoint presentation you've done, and break it down into its component slides. Rewrite word slides so they're no more than eight words each.

Better still, experiment. Try making a presentation or speech without using PowerPoint at all. We did know how to that, even within living memory.

8

The Poetry of the Organization Chart

When I first worked for a large organization, one of the most important documents you could be given was the organization chart.

The chart made sense of the organization. In a large corporation, the org chart demonstrated order, logic, rationality, and control. It provided a compass or map, allowing an employee to navigate the organizational terrain. And it also showed you where you belonged—your box on the chart—and how your group's chart connected to the larger chart to signify your place and how you were part of a much larger whole.

The boxes' positions on the chart were also important. The higher the box, the higher or more important you were in the organization. A chart, done properly, let everyone in the team, group, division, and organization know who fell where. Similar titles could be differentiated by slight differences on the chart. The chart was the physical manifestation of the political pecking order. (At one company I worked for, in the absence of the organization chart, you could determine an individual's grade level by the number of ceiling tiles in his office space or whether a sterling silver water carafe sat on the credenza.)

People actually had jobs for maintaining organization charts. When you work for an organization with 40,000 people (my first company) or 82,000 (my second company), several people could be kept seriously employed keeping all the charts up-to-date.

Like formal poetry, organization charts followed rules, patterns and accepted practice. They possessed an interior rationale; they made sense for both themselves and the organization. You could look at a chart for wildly different functions—the legal department and the maintenance crew for a manufacturing plant, for example—and "read" them with understanding and appreciation.

Then came the 1980s and '90s. Post-modernism wasn't only something that affected university English departments. Two decades of ongoing corporate upheaval meant that organization charts couldn't be changed fast enough; as soon as they were updated, they were out of date. The chart makers often found themselves "de-charted," reorganized, rationalized and downsized out of existence. Almost overnight, the formal poetry of the organization chart—and the organization the chart represented—gave way to a riot of free verse.

The disappearance of organization charts didn't negate the hunger for them; employees still needed charts to make sense of the change around them, to the extent that was possible (and it often wasn't). Paper and then email announcements were a poor substitute for the pages of charts; text could not substitute for the visual representation, and text could hide as much as it communicated. Announcements came too fast about changes too widespread to make sense for any extended period of time.

The organization chart was an expression of hierarchy, the top-down-industrial-mass-production model that prevailed through most of the 20th century. Today most companies model the organization of their personnel after the network, a different kind of poetry altogether, with "nodes" replacing boxes, and pulses of light replacing fixed positions of order.

It makes a kind of sense, this organizational free verse, but many of us remember and still long for the time when we knew where responsibility and accountability lay—expressed by the formal poetry of the organization chart.

Poetic Exercise: If your organization uses a chart of positions and hierarchy, study it. Is it top down, or does responsibility and authority flow in a variety of directions? Would you classify it as a formal poem or free verse? Are all the connecting lines straight or are some "dotted"? Consider the various boxes on the chart—how are they positioned?

If your organization doesn't have a chart of positions, create one yourself. Who reports to whom? How do you indicate responsibility and authority? Is everyone reporting to the supervisor at the same level? If not, how would you indicate differences.

Write a short poem about the organization chart—either the chart your company uses or the one you created yourself.

9

The Poet in the Culture of Control

Businesses, and especially large ones like corporations, have historically been designed to control and manage their environments: minimize risk, reduce occurrences of the unexpected, manage across the supply and production chain, maximize shareowner returns. That model began breaking down in the 1970s, with the extended periods of inflation and disruptions in energy supplies. The 1980s witnessed massive restructurings and reorganizations, which have essentially become institutionalized. At the same time, the electronic communication revolution has changed everything.

But perhaps the most profound change is the one most often overlooked: it is virtually impossible for any organization, private or public, to control its environment. Organizations that believe they still can exercise control have to distort reality, and keep distorting it, to maintain that belief. People can do this, too—for example, when people have to invent and sustain elaborate conspiracy theories to explain facts that conflict with their worldview.

Within organizations desperately trying to hold on to control, creative individuals can often find themselves in a strange position. Their creativity is desperately needed and simultaneously rejected. They can find themselves tagged as "not a team player." It can get worse if they're proven right by external events, which they often are.

Over the years, I've seen this happen, many times. I've experienced this happening. I've watched it happen to others.

"The creative impulse is essentially innovative," poet Luci Shaw writes. "It's always discovering new areas to explore. It experiments. It breaks down old barriers and ventures into new territory. That implies a kind of risk."

If they're not careful, poets shake up the stubborn façade of control and risk job security thanks to their creative, innovative impulse. If anyone knows how to think outside the confines of control—and bring much needed change to the controlling forces that are closed to it—it's the poets.

In the mid-1990s, I asked the IT department for help in creating the company's first website. I was politely refused. "The web is a flash in the pan," I was told. "It's like 8-track tapes. You'll be wasting your money." This was the clincher: "The future is not the web; the future is Lotus Notes."

The person who told me that sincerely believed what he was saying. Behind the statement were huge investments the IT organization had made in Lotus Notes®, including a lot of money and a lot of people (mostly programmers). It was, in other words, a "vested interest." Because of the resources committed, no alternative would be, or could be, considered. The investment effectively controlled how the company perceived and participated in the communication landscape.

Within months, the folly of that commitment had become clear. As it turned out, the web was far more than a flash in the pan; and, in fact, Lotus Notes began to look a lot like 8-track tapes. A new CIO arrived from outside the company and asked who was in charge of web development. He was told, "Well, there is this guy in PR."

Yet in the culture of control, the commitment to Lotus Notes remained stubbornly in place. After a few years of growing dissatisfaction, a "web front-end" was added to make the system work more like the web. It didn't work very well at all, certainly not like the web. In the meantime, because no corporate-wide rule mandated any web activity, people all over the company pursued solutions that utilized websites—eventually creating more than 500.

Clinging to control and resisting change, that company held onto Lotus Notes for more than a decade, sinking untold sums of money into it before finally abandoning it.

They needed to see innovation and act on creative impulse, which is almost impossible in a culture of control. If organizations can loosen their tight grip on functions and those who carry them out just for a little bit—long enough to find a better way—they may find that the ones with the creative impulse—that is, the poets—will see solutions and help that company find the success it's looking for.

Poetic Exercise: If every person who works has one thing in common, it's facing obstacles in getting work done. It may be too much work and too few people to do it, it may be organizational policies and procedures, or it may be someone willfully standing in the way. But we've all faced obstacles.

Consider a time or situation where you faced a serious obstacle to getting your work done. What caused the problem? Was it a clearly identifiable cause (people or policies) or was it something vague and not easily grasped? What did you do (and the options range from working around and overcoming to giving in and walking away)?

In writing, describe the problem, response and outcome in short declarative sentences, no more than ten words each. Now write a poem that describes what happened and its effect on you. And let the words flow.

10

The Poetry of Beauty in the Workplace

If you were asked to identify or name three examples of beauty in your workplace, what would you say?

This would be my response: I have an almost beautiful view from my office window. As I've mentioned, I used to look out over the smoking area. Then the campus went smoke-free. Now I can see a large tree, a garden and a wooded area especially colorful in the fall.

I'm impressed by the gorgeous mural in our cafeteria: huge photographic images of flowers and seashells dominate an entire wall. The wall opposite the mural is glass, looking out to woods.

And in our conference center, a room called the parlor occupies the center of the building. It has mahogany paneling, overstuffed sofas, a writing desk that purportedly belonged to Winston Churchill, and paintings loaned from the local art museum, including a large pastoral landscape over the marble fireplace (the museum has far more works than it can exhibit in its own space). It is a quiet room filled with beautiful things. And it's only meant for sitting; no meetings can be scheduled there.

Note my answers: the view, the physical beauty of art, and the way a room is furnished.

Note what's missing: anything to do with work.

So I ask again, in a different way. Name three examples of beauty in your workplace, and confine your answers to the work itself.

Can work have beauty?

Few of us associate our work with beauty, unless we work in an art museum, florist shop or national park. It's one of the reasons—perhaps the primary reason—we fail to see poetry at work. No beauty, no poetry.

So if I consider my question again, confining my answers to the work itself, I would say this: not all work is beautiful, but all work is meant to have beauty.

I see beauty in a well-researched, well-considered, and well-written article for the company blog.

I see beauty in our news portal, a daily (and sometimes hourly) collection of curated articles about the company and our industry.

I see beauty in a well-argued email.

I see beauty in a regular, and regularly boring, meeting veering into an unexpected group revelation.

I see beauty in the CEO answering well an employee's question at a town hall meeting.

I see beauty in the miracle of the quarterly financial report being published on deadline.

I see beauty in a new employee policy executed flawlessly—and the humanity when it's not.

I see beauty in the commitment of a video team to produce the very best video possible.

I see beauty in the taking of risks, moving beyond conventional wisdom because the idea is right.

I see beauty in the gracious response of the employee who's just been told he's being laid off.

There's more. Much more.

I can cite these as examples because I've experienced every

one of them. I didn't think of them at the time as examples of beauty, but that's what they were.

And each contains a poem. Each has a poetic flow, meter, cadence, and language. Each has an unexpected ending line. Each made me believe that there is great beauty in this life, beauty in my work, and beauty in the work of those around me.

Poetic Exercise: Find the beauty in your workspace—the design, for example, how the space is furnished or decorated, or the framed view from a window.

Then consider the work itself. What could you call beautiful in the actual work that you do? It may be as simple as the way your hand turns a wheel, the sound of a good speaker making a presentation, how suggestions by a number of people came together into an outstanding idea, how a child suddenly understood something you were trying to teach him, even a song playing over the intercom.

Then take the beauty of the workplace and combine it with the beauty of the work you identified. Write the result as a poem.

11

The Poetry of Speechwriting

For most of my career, I've been a speechwriter—that rather ivory-towered function of corporate communications. Most communicators don't like speechwriting. It's not easy to get inside an executive's head and insert words into his or her mouth. And if a speech goes well, the executive, not the speechwriter, gets the credit. If a speech doesn't go well, the speechwriter usually gets all the blame.

Speechwriting is a solitary profession, devoted largely to reading, writing, research, and study. It may be the closest thing we have today to the monastic life outside the monastery, except that at critical stages, the whole world seems to step in. Speechwriting requires ongoing interaction with executives, content experts, librarians, academics, PR people, attorneys, outside consultants, and even other speechwriters. To do it well, the speechwriter must manage all of those people and not let them get in the way of what the executive has to say.

The speechwriter also must understand how ideas, concepts and words translate from the mind to the page or screen, then to the eye and voice, then to the ear, and, if all goes well, to the mind and heart. The speechwriter has to be adept at understanding and working all of these communication "channels."

When I first started writing speeches, I attended seminars and conferences. No one went to college to learn how to be a speechwriter—I stumbled into it like most speechwriters do.

I was working on an issue, some executive needed a speech on the subject, and I became the de facto speechwriter.

What prepared me for speechwriting was poetry.

I loved studying poetry in my high school and college literature classes. I was enchanted with how words could be used and changed to speak to and communicate ideas. I loved the poetic form of Homer and *Beowulf*, Coleridge and Keats, the English poets of World War I, William Butler Yeats and T. S. Eliot. I first read Eliot's "Four Quartets" in high school, and I can remember writing the assigned paper, reading it aloud in class, and even where I bought the volume new for all of 95 cents.

My understanding of poetry at work, however, developed gradually. At the suggestion of a colleague, I began reading poetry regularly to help with speechwriting. I started with the moderns—revisiting Eliot, and adding Wallace Stevens and Dylan Thomas. I followed up "Four Quartets" with "The Love Song of J. Alfred Prufrock" and would later irritate two speechwriting colleagues by reading it aloud in my office cubicle.

That input paid off: poetry helped me write a speech that changed an industry.

Late winter of 1988, I was having trouble finishing a speech—and not just any speech but a significant departure for the company resulting in one of two outcomes: Either the company executive giving it would "elect to pursue career opportunities elsewhere" (companies rarely "fire" senior executives), or the speech would change the company and the industry forever.

The speech needed work. I tried a dozen different endings, and nothing seemed to work.

Then I remembered a television program that had aired on PBS. It was about the Bhopal tragedy in India a few years before, when another company's plant leaked a chemical, killing more than 10,000 people and seriously injuring many more. Understanding what this tragedy had meant to the public was an implicit theme in the speech, and I wondered if I could make it explicit.

In this pre-YouTube era, I ordered a copy of the program and watched it at home. Twice. I took notes. I watched and wiped tears away. Both times.

The program personalized the tragedy. The number of dead and injured was numbing, but the program put names and faces to some of those numbers. The abstract became real. Horrifyingly real.

The speech needed this kind of real.

I watched the program a third time in a conference room at work. As I scattered all my notes and ideas across the conference room table, I saw the poetry of the story that had been staring me in the face.

In longhand, on a yellow legal tablet, I began to write a poem:

Doctors and nurses frantically trying
to learn what had happened,
to know how to treat the victims…
a mother describing how her baby
died in her arms, choking to death…
a young wife watching her husband die…
a 12-year-old boy who was
the only survivor of his large family.
For all our talk about the safety of chemicals,
Bhopal is the end point of chemical risk.

We must live up to what the public expects
of us, and do our jobs as we know we can.
Anything less is failing the trust
we have to the public.
Anything less is failing
ourselves.

As I finished the poem, I knew I had the ending for the speech.

But it was highly emotional. Would the executive be comfortable with it? What would the audience of 1,500 American and British chemical engineers think? How would they respond?

I rewrote the entire draft, working everything to point to the end of the speech, to focus everything on that highly emotional conclusion. The executive read it, nodded, and said, "I think this is it."

The time for the speech arrived. The executive left for London. I had to wait days to hear what happened. When he returned, his secretary called. "He wants to see you, as soon as possible."

My hands were sweating as I arrived at his office. He pointed to the chair in front of his desk. I sat. He didn't say anything at first. Finally, he spoke.

"They cheered," he said. "Fifteen hundred chemical engineers stood and cheered." He paused. "It was like hearing poetry. They want me to record it to send to every engineering chapter in the association."

He smiled again. "They stood and cheered."

The story of a documentary became poetry for a speech that paved the way to an industry's commitment that a tragedy like Bhopal would never happen again. Requests for copies of the speech continued for the next seven years, five years after the executive had retired.

It became known as "the speech that refused to die."

Poetic Exercise: Here are three exercises to try:

1. At some point in our lives, each of has to give a speech or make a presentation. It can be a PowerPoint presentation for a team meeting and it can be a formal speech before thousands. If you've given a speech, pull out the full text, the final slide, or the notes you spoke from. Look at the conclusion and coldly analyze it. Does it sing? Is it memorable? Did it fade away, forgotten? Read the conclusion aloud. Then rewrite it as a poem and read it aloud.

2. Obtain a copy of a recent speech, say, by a business executive, trade association leader, non-governmental organization (NGO), or a government official. Read the speech, and then rewrite the conclusion as a poem. (If nothing else, rewriting it as a poem to be read aloud forces you to put in the "stops" and pauses; as Mark Twain once observed, the most important thing about a speech is knowing when to pause.)

3. This is more involved—find a speech or presentation you've given and write the entire speech out as a poem. This sounds ridiculously hard, but it's actually ridiculously easy, and you can see how poetry can truly benefit an entire speech, not just the ending. Some executives I've worked for required that their "speaking copy" of a speech be in exactly this format. Look what

it does for the beginning of the *Gettysburg Address* (the best way to "see" the difference is to read both versions aloud):

Four score and seven years ago our fathers brought forth on this continent, a new nation, conceived in Liberty, and dedicated to the proposition that all men are created equal.

> Four score
> and seven years ago
> our fathers brought forth
> on this continent
> a new nation
> conceived in Liberty
> and dedicated
> to the proposition
> that all men
> are created equal.

12

The Poetry of Transparency

Concrete.

The word suggests heavy, solid, firm, substantive. (Except in St. Louis, where "concrete" means ice cream.)

One of the characteristics of "stickiness" described by Chip Heath and Dan Heath in *Made to Stick: Why Some Ideas Survive and Others Die*, is concreteness: the idea has to be about something substantive and memorable. Then the Heaths say this: "Concreteness makes targets transparent. Even experts need transparency."

That's a true statement if ever there was one.

The tragedy in Bhopal, India, sent the worldwide chemical industry into a collective shock followed by responses of all kinds—some enlightened, some not. Eventually agreement led to a regulatory response, as the U.S. Congress passed a law with a long name but referred to simply as "Title III."

The law was simple in concept: all manufacturers would have to report emissions of toxic chemicals to air and water, and report it every year. That's all they had to do—report it.

No other action was required. The law was brilliant, because the information wouldn't be stored somewhere out of the way; no, the U.S. Environmental Protection Agency (EPA) would publish the data. The public would get access to it. All of it.

It wasn't only chemical companies that would be reporting. Any company in any industry that used the chemicals on the list would have to report. Chemical companies would have the biggest totals, of course, but a lot of companies no one had ever dreamed used toxic chemicals would have to report, too. Like your local newspaper.

I was working for a chemical company at the time, and it fell to my team to deal with the communications relating to the new law and its implementation. We had about eight months to prepare. We knew from the beginning that we had to convince the company two things would be required.

First, we would disclose our data to the public as soon as we filed it with the EPA, and not wait almost a year for the EPA to report. In other words, we would have to take responsibility for our emissions by disclosing the numbers ourselves, even if everything was legal and under permit.

Second, we would have to make a public commitment to reduce those emissions.

Imagine a group of three poets presenting that message to corporate chieftains.

The first requirement had unassailable logic behind it: if we didn't disclose, the government and everyone who hated chemical companies surely would.

The second drew blank, sometimes hostile stares. More than one executive said that "we will not reduce emissions for the sake of reducing emissions. That's ridiculous." *The same response in presentation after presentation.* Along with a few side comments about the PR department having lost its mind. Well, we thought like poets, and we came up with ideas like this.

We made it all the way to the CEO. He looked at the estimated numbers. He looked at what he knew was likely to happen with public perception. And he said, "We will start with air emissions. We will pledge to reduce our toxic air emissions by 90 percent in four years."

Shocked silence. And then he said, "And then we're going to work on all the other emissions, too. Get busy."

The CEO had not lost his mind along with the PR department. It turns out he was something of a poet himself.

Poetic Exercise: Writing a poem is not a frightening thing; publishing a poem for people to read is another matter. I took major gulps of air before I first published a poem on my blog. Poetry seems to require a certain vulnerability from the poet—putting yourself out there without much defense. Answer these questions: Does poetry demand transparency from the poet? What is it about writing a poem that exposes personal vulnerability in a way that fiction and non-fiction doesn't require?

13

The Poetry of the Crisis

I can't think of anyone working today who doesn't talk about crises at work. Opportunities seem to abound for missteps, mistakes, false impressions, outright distortions, and rumors both false and true. Social media can amplify and in fact create crises for both organizations and individuals, both of whom can also do a good job of creating crises on their own.

At times, it feels like we careen from crisis to crisis, with everything assuming an urgency that demands immediate attention. Important, critical work is set aside to deal with crises, sometimes never to be touched again. I once had a boss who referred to this as "the tyranny of the urgent at the expense of the important."

While crises are usually different, each crisis may share common elements with others, like unexpectedness; an urgency to do something even if it's not clear what the something is; a difference of opinions within the organization as to what to do; an overreliance on legal counsel (or influence); and a tendency to feed on each other, leading to a "crisis mentality" or "crisis culture" for managing work.

Where crises differ is in their immediate cause, the people involved, and the lessons to be learned. Some crises are one-off, never to be repeated. Others, in the repetition, reflect something fundamentally flawed in the organization.

Crises are the poetry of surprise, upset, and human frailty. They are often the poetry of organizational change, the poetry of disruption of the status quo. They can speak powerfully to an organization's managers and people, and they can also fall on deaf ears. Crises expose our humanity, both flawed and good; our limitations and potential reach; our courage, and our fears. And they do all of these things simultaneously.

A light movement of wind,
a small ripple in the water,
a comment, a tweet, a post,
a few words, and it begins.
A storm, a tsunami,
a hurricane, an eruption
sudden and unexpected,
a crash, and it begins.
Back to normal becomes
a place of no return.

It's difficult to see when you're in the thick of a crisis, but you can look for the poetry that's there, because it is there. You can see it in the themes, the metaphors, the rhythm and flow, what words are used and how they are used. And finding the poetry in the crisis will suggest the path forward.

Some years ago, I was involved in dealing with an online hoax. A group had created a counterfeit website, one that looked like the real thing and even linked correctly to all the other parts of the actual company's website. The only hint that something was off was in the URL—it was obviously different. The page contained an announcement that wasn't true. Many people, thinking it was true, were posting about it on Twitter, Facebook, and blogs. Some news organizations, believing it legitimate, posted it on their sites.

Crisis time.

We dealt with it by moving fast and aggressively. The crisis and the fake announcement that caused it contained their own interior logic and rhythms, as did the resolution of the crisis. The flow of work became a kind of narrative poem, recited and explained so many times that it became a kind of epic. For some time after, the entire episode became a referral point for dealing with crises.

Crises are not all that uncommon. Organizations experience all kinds of crises—financial, accidents, deaths of executives, labor issues, downsizings and restructurings, product failures, cash flow shortfalls, fraud, environmental disasters. Sometimes the sheer volume of what has to be accomplished can become something of a crisis.

As much as we might complain about lurching from crisis to crisis—or the workplace characterized by crises—crises actually help "edit" the workplace. What's important becomes obvious, focusing the attention of the entire organization like a laser so that appropriate resources are immediately applied.

Crises simplify and clarify.

Much like a poem.

A part of the company I was working for—the business that was the old heartland of the enterprise—was being spun off. The people going with the spin-off fully understood the meaning. No matter what anyone might say, companies don't spin off operations or businesses that are highly profitable, with long-term prospects for success. No, companies spin off businesses that "no longer fit the portfolio," won't produce the desired level of profit, or—best-case scenario—will just chug along at a less-than-desirable return on investment.

The new company had nine months to create an organization, find a new name, fight over assets, select management teams, file a raft of legal documents, apply for stock registration, and prepare employees for a new world. Management was struggling over the best way to launch the company. No one felt like celebrating. The situation felt more like a funeral than a birth.

The poet was asked to figure it out.

And the poet said, "We're going to have a party."

"Engineers and research scientists don't party," said the soon-to-be CEO, himself an engineer.

And the poet said, "Trust me," displaying a confidence he didn't have.

The poet did not write a kickoff script, embedded with key messages, vision and mission statement. Instead, the poet wrote a poem, an epic poem, mostly in prose format, celebrating the heroic. A band was hired, as was an emcee. A plan was designed for a round-the-world "join-up," where each location would work around complicated time zones to celebrate the new company for two minutes in their local language.

Reviewing the plan, the CEO said, "Engineers don't party."

"I think they will," the poet replied. "Trust me," he said. And he promptly found a private place to throw up.

Guidelines for all the location parties were developed. Every cake had the same company logo. Every employee would receive a work shirt with the logo—the same shirt, the world over. Technical arrangements ensured every connection would be connected.

The poet did a final review with the CEO. "I know," the poet said. "Engineers don't party."

The CEO nodded. "That's exactly right. This will end badly. But I know what you're going to say. 'Trust me.'"

The official spin-off day arrived. The poet arrived very early. The balloon drops were in place ("But if this blows up don't drop those balloons"). The band arrived. The technicians were in place. The emcee did a few practice runs. Phone and video connections were checked and double-checked. An unexpected crisis with a location in the United Kingdom was fixed. People began arriving. The epic poem was beginning.

The emcee was perfect. The band was perfect. The CEO communicated enthusiasm and excitement that the poet didn't think he had in him. The round-the-world join-up went without a hitch, and everyone heard people speaking English, Portuguese, Spanish, Chinese, Japanese, French, Italian, and a dozen others.

Celebration Central at headquarters began to rock. Hundreds of people were dancing around the stage. And the poet was stunned to see the CEO and the COO (another engineer) square-dancing together on the dais, in full view of the video cameras.

Engineers knew how to party after all.

And dance.

The epic poem had come to life.

Poetic Exercise: Think back to a workplace crisis in which you were involved (or perhaps one that's happening now). Briefly outline it, identifying its component parts, underlying cause (there are always underlying causes), the catalyst that set it into motion, the organization's response, the outcome, and the organization's lessons learned. The response to a crisis is often multifaceted, and the outcome can be unexpected. Some people will behave like heroes, and some people won't. And an organization may learn little or nothing and thus increase its vulnerability or enhance the possibility of another crisis.

All of this is the stuff of poetry (not to mention a good novel). Analyzing and studying to reap every possible benefit and insight—that's what poets do with every aspect of life. They analyze and reap truth and insight from life experiences, then express the essence of each truth and insight. Look at your notes, and focus on one aspect to write a poem about.

With poem in hand, ask yourself, What did considering the crisis in this way teach me? Can I write a poem about dealing with the next crisis?

14

The Poetry of Interpersonal Conflict

The workplace, like the rest of the world we live in, is a mixture of the good and bad, of nobility of purpose and unbridled ambition, of supportive encouragement and backstabbing politics. If you get more than two people in a room, you have the ingredients for conflict, politics, and factions. Working in high-pressure workplaces only intensifies this tendency for conflict (additionally fueled by intra-office email).

To make sense of this, and sometimes to seek a resolution, I write poems. From what I hear from friends and colleagues, this could become an entire genre of poetry—the poetry of workplace conflict.

I don't write nasty little darts aimed at superiors, subordinates, or colleagues, and I keep these artistic expressions off Twitter or Facebook where I've witnessed colleagues battle it out with each other on their Facebook pages. Instead, I try to think through what might be at the heart of the matter, reflect on it, and then begin to understand it by writing a poem or series of poems.

I've done this when (1) someone was unjustifiably laid off; (2) the workplace became overwhelming; (3) a conflict (not necessarily involving me) broke into the open or, even worse, stayed disruptively hidden; (4) dealing with a career disappointment; (5) dealing with a career success, which can be even more of a problem than a disappointment; (6) people used their titles or positions to force their desired path or outcome, even when it was the wrong choice; (7) meetings going on behind closed doors resulted in bad decisions; and (8) resources were over-allocated to one area while another area starved.

Poetry helped me process and express each scenario. I've found that poetry gets to the heart of just about any kind of challenge or problem in the workplace and reveals important lessons, realities, and universal truths.

For example, I've been surprised at how much workplace conflict is driven by fear: Fear of someone seeming smarter or more capable. Fear of embarrassment. Fear of what may happen if we accept responsibility. Fear of making a mistake. Fear of failure. Fear of loss of respect or position. Fear of doing something new or different.

All of us experience these very human fears. All of us have been affected, sometimes overwhelmed, by these fears. Poetry—the reading and writing of a poem—can often help identify these fears and how they motivate us and others.

Capturing workplace issues and expressing them through poetry helps diminish anxiety and angst, resulting in a calming effect. As I funnel thoughts and fears through pen and keyboard (I prefer a pen for a first draft), I often begin to view tense and intense situations with a calmer, clearer perspective.

Few jobs today are stress-free or even low-stress. People must work despite limited resources, limited staff, organizational politics and conflicts, reorganizations and layoffs, clashes between work and family demands, the speed and volume of information (and how it's delivered). Workplace stress has been the new normal for at least the last two decades, and I'm old enough to know it wasn't always this way.

We relieve stress in different ways. We exercise. We pursue unusual hobbies or avocations. We travel (involving its own kind of stress, especially at airports). We quit organizational work life. And we drink, overeat, get sick and sometimes die from stress. Recently, I had the painful experience of a ruptured disk in my back; my doctor connected it directly to stress in my job.

We cope as best we can. But why not turn to poetry? I've found that poetry helps reduce stress at work, in five specific ways.

1. Read Poetry • Reading a single poem is easily manageable. *Every Day Poems*, a subscription service through *Tweetspeak Poetry*, makes it easy by delivering an excellent poem a day by email. In addition to *Every Day Poems,* I read poets—new and old, dead and living—to the extent my schedule allows. Sometimes I peruse only a poem or two; other times, I dive into a book of poems in one sitting.

Reading poetry does several things for me. It focuses my mind away from the immediate stresses in my work life. It presents an idea, subject, or theme entirely apart from my usual work experience, challenging my mind to think differently. And reading poetry moves me to a different means of expression by presenting its ideas in an unexpected format. Reading a poem costs nothing in terms of commitment or action—though you may feel inspired to let it impact you in that way.

2. Take a Poem Apart • I start with a poem, usually a short one, and "explicate" it (the official term for analyzing a poem): Why does this poem start that way? What images does it evoke? Why are phrases used that way? Why use that word, when another would have been sufficient or even better? What idea is it trying to convey, and does it work? Or could it work better some other way?

3. Speak Poetry • It's tempting to think I understand a poem when I read it silently, but when I read it aloud, my understanding can change—human speech combining with written words can transform meaning and understanding. Speaking a poem out loud can also offer a soothing rhythm—eddies of calm in a chaotic work day.

4. Listen in Poetry • No matter what kind of job we have, at one time or another we find ourselves in meetings. My job takes me to lots of meetings. About two years ago, I started "listening in poetry" at these meetings and presentations, even taking notes structured like poems.

Writing notes like poems allows me to chunk statements and ideas, organize my thoughts, and structure my responses. It makes the time spent in meetings more productive and interesting, and even allows me to feel a kind of positive rebellion against the interaction by feeling my role as poet. The easiest way to try this is with the ubiquitous PowerPoint presentation—look at bullet points as lines in a poem and edit accordingly.

5. Write Poetry • Sometimes I write poetry to deal with workplace stress. Organizational work life can provide great fodder for poems. For example, I'll take a problem, conflict, success or failure I'm wrestling with and write it out as a poem. If nothing else, expressing the situation, interaction, or event in poetic form helps me make sense of it.

Poetry is not a cure-all for workplace stress. But it is one constructive way to deal with it, and cheaper than doctors, physical therapy and psychiatrists. And perhaps it can help produce something good from the stress—something in the form of a poem.

Poetic Exercise: Try using poetry to explain and understand a problem or challenge in your workplace. See what happens. Select one in which you were personally involved. Pour the emotion, fear, hurt and anger onto the page (remember, no one else has to see this).

Then write a poem about the same situation from the opposing perspective—imagine and compose the poem in the voice of another person or group involved.

It may not resolve the problem immediately, but your understanding will increase.

Take Your Poet to Work Day

Take Your Poet to Work Day, created by *Tweetspeak Poetry*, occurs once a year on the third Wednesday in July. It's caught on in Australia, Holland, the United States and a few places in between. *The Atlantic* promoted it. And *The Paris Review*. And the Poetry International Festival Rotterdam.

The idea behind the first Take Your Poet to Work Day was to select one of the conveniently-created cartoon cutouts of Eliot, Dickinson, Poe, Neruda, Teasdale, Rumi or Basho, print it, cut it out, color it, paste it to a stick, and then insert your poet somewhere in your workspace. And maybe tell a story.

Doris Alderink, RN, BSN, PCCN, took a cutout of Emily Dickinson (taped to a popsicle stick) to the cardiovascular unit of the hospital where she works. Emily was literally in the heart of it all because Doris wedged the stick into the aorta of the plastic model heart displayed at the nurse's station.

"I didn't know any of her poems," Doris said, "so I just went online and printed some off to post on the board. I brought in the popsicle-stick-Emily and we read about her—nobody knew anything about her—and it provided an avenue of conversation that we would not normally have in that kind of environment."

She said several people could still remember a few lines from poems they had learned in school, like "Paul Revere's Ride," "Song of Hiawatha," and Rudyard Kipling's "If." That conversation led to a discussion of Edgar Allan Poe, several people recalling his short story "The Tell-Tale Heart"—an appropriate title for the staff of a cardiovascular unit.

This simple act of inviting poetry into the workplace created a sideline conversation—even laughter—that lasted all day. "Who thinks about Emily Dickinson?" Doris laughed. "Most people don't, so Take Your Poet to Work Day was kind of uncharted territory for us. Poetry is not a normal part of our world, but everyone received it warmly. It was fun."

While I don't do cutouts (yet), I did bring some poets to work (via their books): Wallace Stevens (a favorite), Billy Collins (close to a favorite), Wendell Berry (a favorite though we have some political differences), and Edgar Lee Masters (who has been the favorite since high school and given the fact he's lasted this long as my favorite, it's unlikely he will be dethroned anytime soon).

I brought my then-current issue of *Poetry* magazine to work as well. The issue included three poems by Scott Cairns and one by James Galvin, among others; an article by the late film critic

Roger Ebert; and four remembrances, including one of Richard Wilbur by former poet laureate Donald Hall.

I inserted the four books directly into my workspace, and in one way or another, all four of these poets, and a few others, helped me understand the poetry in work—and poetry at work.

15

The Poetry of the Best Job You Ever Had
(or the Worst)

You're interviewing for a job. The interviewer asks, "What's the best job you ever had?" Employment consultants will tell you that the ideal answer is, "The one I have now." But that begs the question, "Then why do you want to leave it?" A more creative, confident answer may work better, so I suggest thinking back to previous work experiences and tapping them for material that can be expressed with hints of poetry in the next interview.

I can think of three that could tie for the best job I ever had.

Managing editor for my college newspaper: The editor got the editorial page and all the glory; the managing editor got all the responsibility for the rest of the newspaper. All the editors, reporters, and photographers reported to me—a real-time adrenaline rush, five days a week, assigning stories, covering breaking news, finding myself in the middle of student protests (reporting, not protesting), getting calls from top university officials. I wouldn't have a job of that level of responsibility and importance for another fifteen years. The poetry from this position exuded energy.

Helping lead a corporate environmental revolution: I wrote a speech, and then another, and then another. A major environmental issue invited corporate change, and the company I was working for ultimately seized it. We turned the industry upside down. Executives inside the company accused the speechwriters of running the corporation. Who, me? What? Even in the workplace, poets are often accused of being revolutionaries, sparking and igniting change through the power of their ideas expressed through precisely chosen words. The work of a poet isn't to run things, but to reveal what others struggle to see and, sometimes, to convey poetically and powerfully what needs to be done.

The PR guy for an urban school district: A governmental upheaval occurred when an outside management firm was brought in to restructure an urban school district. They hired me to be the communications guy. Think downsizings, school closings, massive organizational change, protests—all on top of normal, everyday life in an urban school district. I was in the news media several times a day, five days a week—sometimes seven days a week. One TV station tracked me down on a Saturday for an interview—at the car dealership where I was getting maintenance work done on my car. This job provided me with quick-thinking skills to communicate the situation as clearly and concisely as possible—excellent training for a poet at work.

As much as I loved those opportunities, the reality is the best jobs we've ever had can also be the worst jobs we've ever had. All three of those jobs I just listed would also make the "worst job" list. Excitement, constant change, and adrenaline rushes can lead to burnout. But when I started writing poems, I began to understand that good and bad, and best and worst, often walk hand in hand. Contradictions exist within the same setting or situation. Finding a way to acknowledge this reality and express it, through poetry, freed me to embrace the contradictions.

Although writing poetry comes close to speechwriting— that is, good speechwriting—a poem can convey ambiguity in a way that speechwriting cannot. Unlike a speech that addresses questions and offers solutions, poetry usually avoids answers and instead poses more questions—even forcing the reader (and poet) to live with those questions. A poem requires you to look at a subject or a theme from a very different angle; a poet can shed more light or create fog where most people think clarity rules.

It's only 9 a.m.
Channel 5 is waiting, cameras
filming in expectation
of a statement, any statement,
it doesn't matter what it says;
school board members
are leaking emails on each other,
the teacher on the phone
is correcting my pronunciation;
the newspaper uses police radios
to follow the school district news
while the consultant is calling
about "a better brand for the schools";
the parents' protest is scheduled
for 5:30; the mayor's office
is sending PR instructions
and I'm told the teachers have
a sick-out today because they
can't bank sick days anymore
and it's only 9 a.m. and
my first day on the job. I'm
going to love this place.

Poetic Exercise: What's the best job you've ever had? Write down the reasons for your answer. Then write down what you didn't like about it—a scheming colleague, a forgetful boss, long hours, disruptions to family life. No job is perfect; every job is a mix of the good and bad.

Now take your lists and write a poem, alternating lines between good and bad.

16

The Poetry of Unemployment

At the end of 1999, I found myself the recipient of "the package"—the severance package that goes along with the legal document you need to sign if you accept the package. The document includes a commitment not to sue. One of the Human Resources people, forgetting I was "on the list" and could translate the jargon, wandered around chirping how the package "met the test." The test was not some government standard of non-discrimination; the test was actually whether or not the company got sued.

I waited until 55 minutes before the 45-day deadline to sign and deliver. The chirrupy HR person was nearly prostrate with anxiety, and with good reason: my attorney looked at the people on the list and said, "One female, 94 males, all between the ages of 40 and 50. This is so discriminatory it reeks. You could win this case, and easily. But you'd have to tie up your life for the next three to four years. And they know that."

There was poetry in there, somewhere. But I couldn't write poetry then and find it difficult even now. Organizations think of layoffs as "business" decisions; the people affected find them intensely personal and painful. Layoffs most often are management failures.

Even years later, this remains intensely personal for me. And painful. But unemployment is part of work and, therefore, offers its own poetry.

A few years back, I worked for a company heading into a restructuring after not experiencing one for a long time. More than half of the work force had joined the company since the last layoff. Anxiety and fear of the unknown were off the charts.

We decided to blog the restructuring (see chapter 17).

We published a series of four posts, all written by the only person on staff who had gone through a restructuring (me). I simply explained how restructurings work, how decisions are made, what happens to people who are affected and what happens to people who aren't. This wasn't a senior-level executive trying to be reassuring; this was an employee who had gone through the experience. The posts included advice on how to deal with people who were laid off, things that could lessen anxiety, what outplacement services were like, and how to explain your situation to family and friends.

The posts set records for readership that still haven't been surpassed. I received numerous emails from employees thanking me for being honest. And the company got credit for allowing an employee to talk candidly about what a restructuring and downsizing were like.

Countless books have been written on how to deal with being fired or laid off. I haven't read them all, but I've read a number of them. They generally contain helpful advice but didn't resonate with me as profoundly as a poem by Richard Cole.

A professional business writer in Austin, Texas, Cole wrote "October Layoffs" to relive the experience of unemployment, at once familiar and painful, speaking far more profoundly and memorably to me on the topic than that stack of nonfiction books:

October Layoffs

I

Working in a troubled office, you develop
a fine ear for door slams, like the managerial
"Now see here!" — righteous and swift.
But you also distinguish the other kind,
still forceful but touched with a miserable hint
of reluctance that says, "I truly hate
to do this, but I'm your boss."

II

Sitting at my desk, heart pounding,
almost in tears, I listen to our supervisor
talking rapidly next door. I put my ear to the wall,
and I hear Pat say, "Well, I figured ..."

III

Full moon, October. I lie awake
half dreaming, drifting, and I see myself
making the rounds at the office, saying
goodbye, hugging each person in turn.
"You've done a good job. Be proud."
Then immediately another image:
I'm sitting tailor fashion on my desk,
literally in burlap and ashes, head lowered,
my collar open, cool air on my neck.

A broad ax rises. I lower my head some more,
and the ax slices easily through my neck.
I feel my head tip forward
and fall, blood washing my chest,
soaking my shirt.

Startled, I lie in the dark. I've seen,
I think, what I needed to see:
that I'll never work again for anyone else,
not with my heart, not with faith,
and I close my eyes, falling asleep
and sleep like the dead until morning.

That slice. Not one management book could capture through prose the shock of that slice. Despite the power of this poem to express the impact of losing one's job, the poet leaves the reader in limbo. Because the fact is that morning comes. We may "sleep like the dead," but morning comes. And the story of waking up is another poem to live and write. In my case, I went to work for myself for the next three-and-a-half years; I needed a break from formal organizations, though I eventually went back, stopping first in education before returning to the corporate world.

The time away from working within an organization felt like a sabbatical taken while still working. I learned much about human nature, good and bad. I learned much about myself. The ideas for what would eventually become two novels were born during this time. Good things can come of difficult experiences, and poetry can help by painting an accurate picture of human nature, and ourselves.

Cole's poems found in his collections *The Glass Children* (1986) and *Success Stories: Poems and Essays* (1998) convey this same understanding, this same self-knowledge. Something is always broken or lost when one loses a job or when a colleague loses a job. I've never heard of any organization "doing it well" when it comes to layoffs, but we can choose to come out of the experience better and wiser, and that's what his poems suggest.

Poetic Exercise: If you've experience being laid off, write down what happened. Try to recall all the different components: if or how the rumors started; how the organization communicated before, during, and after; how you actually learned about your own situation and what your immediate reaction was; how you told your family; and what you did to start developing a new way apart from the workplace you knew.

17

The Poet Blogs the Layoff

At work in 2009, we started blogging on our internal website about coming layoffs.

It was part of the Great Recession of 2008-2010 (and remnants keep stubbornly hanging on). The announcement of impending layoffs had been made, and then came silence. Decisions would be announced two months later. In the meantime, fear entered the workplace.

At one time, silence for two months would have been the official policy. But organizational silence no longer works. The Internet, social media, and new workplace expectations and realities have swept away most of the old organizational policies. Announce a layoff, and expect to see it tweeted on Twitter or discussed on Facebook. The employer-employee contract died in the 1980s. We may yearn for the days of two-way loyalty, but those days have passed. There's only forward.

One of the things my team was responsible for at the time was the corporate intranet, including news and blogs. We talked about what to do. If we can't answer people's most important question—do I have a job?—could we at least indicate it was okay to talk about it?

My people knew I had been laid off from a job with another company in 1999. They asked what had happened and what I'd experienced. I told them.

One of them said, "Can you blog it? Can you blog what happened to you?"

Well, sure, I could do that. I could also anticipate possible reactions and repercussions.

But then I thought about all of the people and families worrying about the what-ifs at home, seeing the lousy economic news getting worse. If I blogged my own experience, it wouldn't answer their critical questions, but it might say it's okay to talk about it, and that we all shared the same fears and concerns.

The poet in me won out.

I talked with my boss and peers. I got the green light. I blogged. It was the equivalent of writing a series of difficult poems. Even ten years after the fact, much of it still felt raw. I would be exposing something to thousands of people—something of myself.

But this is what poets do. And this is what I did.

The first post was about what happened to me in 1999—how it happened and how I reacted. And what I did to prevent the layoff from controlling me.

The second post was about the questions I got from my family. I talked about shame, embarrassment, feelings of inadequacy, and questions from my children (like "Didn't you work hard enough? Do we have to move?"). And then came the ultimate understanding that my job, and the loss of my job, did not define my value. Something else defined my worth, and that was my faith. Because my faith defined who I was, and because I tried to practice my faith at church, at home and on the job, it was my response to my layoff that defined who I was.

The third blog post was the most heart wrenching—about a layoff when I wasn't affected, but a close friend was.

In 1992, a close friend learned he was losing his job. When he called to tell me, my confident, focused, intense friend sounded devastated, depressed and ashamed. And the situation was even worse than it appeared.

We met in the company cafeteria the next day. I was waiting for him at a table. He walked over, lunch tray in his hands, and stood there.

"Are you sure you want to be seen with me?" he asked.

I thought he was joking. He wasn't. His entire department had stopped speaking to him. He had to stay in the office for the next 45 days, while being shunned.

I was stunned. So I did the only think I knew to do. I stood and hugged him. He cried. What a scene that made, right there in the cafeteria.

Years after it had happened, I blogged that story. I wrote that I had promised myself when this happened that I would never do to anyone what had been done to my friend. And I urged the readers of my blog post seventeen years later to make the same promise. I said that I knew it was awkward, but if you didn't know what to say to friends who had just lost their jobs, try this: "How can I help you?" And help them network, be a reference, make some phone calls, and follow up with them later.

In other words, love them as yourself. The odds are good that you will be one of them someday, and you may need someone to love you.

I can't say my blog posts went viral, but within three days more than 2,500 people had read the first post. Comments got posted. One employee published a story himself. I received emails, phone calls and visits. People stopped and thanked me in the cafeteria. The reactions were fairly uniform: it's okay to talk about this; it's okay to talk about what we're afraid of. We're in this together.

The day after the first post, the company operator called me, asking me where to direct a reporter who was calling about a story. I gave her the name and number. She thanked me, and then hesitated.

"I read your blog." She paused. "It was good." She paused again. "Thank you."

Layoffs not only affect the people who lose their jobs. They also affect the people who remain. And I'm not talking about so-called "survivor guilt." No, what usually follows a layoff program is reorganization, changes in workloads, changes in team structure and often changes in team leaders.

Layoffs and reorganizations are hard, every day. Existing ways of doing work have been disrupted. Close colleagues may be gone. People you considered friends no longer come to work. You may find yourself in the outplacement center.

In these painful, confusing times, opening up honest lines of communication feels like inviting the simplicity and directness of poetry to speak into hard places; in other ways, the poetry at work stops, and time has to pass before it begins again.

Poetic exercise: If you've been laid off, survived a layoff, or had a close friend or relative laid off, you know how strong the emotions can run. Strong emotions won't do much for your sleep, but they can contribute to some fine poems.

Write a poem from the perspective of the supervisor having to tell an employee that he's being laid off. Remember what led to the decision how the plan came together; the legal and human resources considerations; how the individual was told and the response; how you communicated to those not directly involved.

18

The Poetry of Electronic Work

Twenty years ago, I sat through a series of meetings with the company's IT people. We wanted to create an email newsletter for employees; IT resisted. "It will crash the system," we were told. "This will harm all of our computer systems," they said. I even heard vague hints that overtaxing the email system could lead to financial chaos and cultural collapse in the West.

It sounds rather quaint today, but in 1993, email was just beginning to gain acceptance. My company had reached the mark of 5,000 employees on email. With close to 45,000 total staff, we figured we reached critical mass. We knew of only two other employee email newsletters in North America at the time: at AT&T and an insurance company in Canada. Neither was a good role model; the insurance company's newsletter crossed multiple computer platforms and systems, like ours did, but had a much smaller distribution. AT&T's employee reach dwarfed ours, and they were on one universal computer platform. We generally followed the path set by the insurance company.

After months of meetings with IT, we had one of those light bulb moments. No one could technically stop us from starting our newsletter, short of shutting the system down. The technology sat there, tempting us. "You don't need permission," it whispered. "You can just do it."

We had both poets and bureaucrats on our team. We argued what we should do.

The poets won. We took the risk and launched our newsletter. Nothing bad happened. In fact, the email system handled the newsletter just fine. Nothing even minor happened.

The first lesson we learned was to look at dire claims of disaster with a skeptical eye. The second lesson was that an email newsletter was work. Despite the appearance of ease that bytes and pixels seemed to promise, nothing was easy about composing and distributing an email newsletter. And the third lesson we learned was that when employees liked the newsletter (and they did), it soon made its way far outside the company—they forwarded the newsletter to friends, sales prospects, academics, family members and just about anyone else they thought might find it interesting.

That was the fourth lesson we learned: in an electronic world, internal communication ends up as external communication, erasing natural barriers.

The fifth lesson: electronic communication operates a lot like speech. Many of us have learned to our embarrassment that email is not like a short handwritten note—the note sits on a desk whereas email can travel and be understood in very different ways, especially if you hit "reply all" instead of "reply." And most of us have learned not to SHOUT on Twitter and Facebook.

Most of my current job's day-to-day work involves Twitter, Facebook, YouTube, discussion boards, and a blog. To do them right in an organizational setting is labor intensive—even more time-consuming than in a personal setting, because I have to consider both internal and external sensibilities as I manage these channels.

Like all work, the work of electronic communications contains inherent poetry, perhaps several inherent poetries: the poetry of information, the poetry of relationship, the poetry of psychology. And, like the poetry of several other disciplines, it is also the poetry of encouragement and affirmation while simultaneously being the poetry of conflict, debate, and acrimony. In few other areas do so many kinds of poetry come together and fuse as they do in the electronic communications of online communities. And it is some of the hardest work I've ever done.

People will say things on Twitter and Facebook that they would never dream of saying in person. Many of us have come to believe that online communities offer some degree of anonymity and security when actually they do not (ask the National Security Administration, or the people who set up fake Facebook accounts). This leads to online communities that express the poetry of extremes. We scream in ALL CAPS. We suggest sarcasm with LOL. We use pictures and emoticons to illustrate our emotions. We use profanity to an astonishing degree.

At the same time, we create things of great beauty, lasting relationships, profound thinking and words that affirm and encourage. *Tweetspeak Poetry* was born on Twitter, and I personally find it a place of both insight and beauty.

The poetry of electronic work is a song, a song of myself (to borrow from one poet) that joins with hundreds and thousands of other songs. It is a chorus of the sacred and the profane, the individual and the common.

It's not that I tweet,
therefore I am, or that

I like, therefore I belong
to a tribe whose sustenance
is bytes and jpegs, ALL CAPS
and LOLs; IMHO* it is that
I am, therefore I tweet.

*IMHO = In My Humble Opinion

Poetic Exercise: If you have an account on Twitter, look at your last ten tweets. First, eliminate the "thanks for the RT" posts. Look at some of the things you've actually been tweeting. And then fashion a poem using the words of those ten tweets. (And watch for periodic announcements from *Tweetspeak Poetry* about poetry jams: tweetspeakpoetry.com.)

Now do the same thing using two or three emails you've written. Read the resulting poems aloud.

If you're feeling rather bold, consider posting your poems on Facebook, or your blog if you have one. Invite comment.

Using Work to Block Creativity

You will never hear any organization—business, government, non-profit (including religious)—say that creativity has no value. No one posts a sign over the door that says "Abandon creativity, all who enter here" or "Leave your imagination at the door."

Yet, as an executive I once wrote speeches for always said, "Policy is what you do, not what you say."

The fact is, organizational settings like to strangle creativity in the cradle. I might even go so far as to say that most workplaces want work instead of creativity—even if creativity will save money. Workplaces like workaholics, encouraging people to work so long and hard that they live their jobs, staying sixteen hours a day (and longer).

I know this. I speak from experience. And I can't say I'm completely free of the addiction.

As Julia Cameron points out in *The Artist's Way: A Spiritual Path to Higher Creativity,* workaholism is a self-inflicted block on creativity among several, including food, alcohol, dry and desert-like times, fame, sex, and even competition with your peers.

I once worked at a place that offered a toxic combination of these things, expecting long hours and competition among colleagues resulting in the inevitable backstabbing and politics. The most proficient politicians were promoted. A "blame culture" prevailed, in which taking risk, trying new things and stepping outside a very small comfort zone were all discouraged.

Not surprisingly, the company stayed in continual reorganization.

In that environment, the choices were to go with the flow or go against the flow. Both could be done. Both had costs.

Creativity can threaten an organization because it leads to change, upending carefully-constructed political systems, and threatening someone's perceived influence and power. Poets, if they remain creative, can find themselves as road kill on the organizational highway.

But creativity is equally threatening to individuals, including those of us who try to practice it, and for very similar reasons: it leads to change, upsetting the way we're used to doing things, and forcing a sense of honesty when we'd prefer to remain ignorant.

So you take refuge in workaholism. You work harder. You pay less attention to your family and friends. You don't volunteer at church or with the local scouting troop. You bury yourself in a busyness that is only the appearance of work. You lose the poetic way of seeing the world and processing life. You no longer hear the rhythms of the meetings and spot the patterns in the workplace.

Blame "the office," management, colleagues or all of the above, but we are the ones making the choice. And we will choose the creativity block of workaholism to seek a benefit of some kind: safety, security, maintaining the status quo, avoiding painful decisions, preserving our empire or any of a host of other things we tell ourselves we need or want.

But this is not the way it's meant to be, and deep down, we know it. It takes the courage of a poet to set us free to seek creativity once more. Is it in you?

19

The Poetry of Workplace Restoration

My job takes place almost entirely in the digital world: Facebook, Twitter, YouTube, blogs, websites, email, online news and trade publications, webinars, online meetings, phone conferences. I am in virtual Mumbai one moment and Missouri, the next. I rarely share the physical presence of many of the people I work directly with—people in offices in Buenos Aires, São Paulo, Mexico City, Brussels, London, Washington, and Calgary.

It's fast-paced work, often hectic, sometimes resembling the frenzy of Wall Street or the Chicago Board of Trade. Most times it's straightforward work, carried out in a rhythm and pace like that of most other workplaces. A few times, it's like wading through a swamp, dealing with the dark side of the human condition. People will say anything, reveal anything, and sometimes threaten anything that they would never dream of doing face-to-face. At least, that's my hope.

When I'm wading through the swamp, I turn to poetry.

First, I'll take a few minutes and read several poems or reread one poem several times. The reading hollows out a space of quiet and solitude in the middle of online crises, ringing phones, urgent emails, harsh tweets and endless meetings. I find it restorative.

Twisted and pulled,
attacked and abraded,
the mind, the heart

turn to a few labored lines,
reveling in the offered solace.

Second, because I do a lot of online writing, I'll turn my back on the computer, mute the phone, close the office door, and work on writing assignments using poetic form. A blog post about a customer begins as a poem. A news summary starts its life in rhyming couplets. A tweet for the company begins as a 140-character poem. An email that deals with a particularly difficult problem begins as a poem, each line focused on different aspects of the issue. In those times, poetry offers clarity, allowing me to reduce all the extraneous and ancillary thoughts to a few simple statements. It focuses me on the precise message I need to express.

It's reductionist, it is,
distilling what swirls
in the mind's maelstrom
into a mere handful
of simplicity.

Third, because I work across channels, with information flowing in and out and across on a constant basis, work can easily slip towards chaos and confusion. We playfully (or perhaps accurately) call this "exploding head syndrome," but there's a serious side to it—you forget what channel is being worked, mistakes can be made, and the mind has a tendency to shut down. The work requires speed and accuracy.

I turn to poetry for help in organizing. I flip a switch in my head and start processing information like I'm processing a poem, understanding the way the thoughts are flowing and how the words are used. After I became used to doing this, I began to "see" the poetry in the flow of communication around my team and me. I avoided chaos and confusion by identifying the rhyme and reason, and thinking of the messages as poetry allows me to find it, identify it, then shape it into the work that needs to be done.

> In the beginning was
> the chaos, formless yet
> pulsating with life,
> demanding almost
> pleading for reality
> defined.

The fourth way I use poetry at work is to cure burnout.

Any kind of work can lead to burnout, which can hit not only after weeks of sustained and frenzied effort but also daily, because the work doesn't stop, and creativity has to flow whether or not a person is brain-dead and burned out.

When I'm feeling drained, I turn to a 1940 edition of an old English textbook, *Prose and Poetry of America*, edited by H. Ward McGraw. It's missing the latest seventy years of American literature, but it contains enough to meet the need—Emerson, Longfellow, Poe, Whitman, Dickinson, Edwin Arlington Robinson, Amy Lowell, Frost, Edna St. Vincent Millay, Sandburg, Teasdale, Joyce Kilmer, and many others. Also sitting on my office bookshelf is my high school senior English textbook, *England in Literature* (published in 1963) and several collections of speeches, the best of which sound like poetry.

I read from these, preferably aloud, with my office door

closed. I can envision myself fighting with Henry V at Agincourt, sitting with Joyce Kilmer under one of his trees, or reading tombstones with Edgar Lee Masters at the cemetery in Spoon River.

I find inspiration in reading these words that awaken my deadened mind, soften my dulled heart, and invigorate my psyche to move through burnout into a brighter, bolder reality.

That's how I use poetry at work: to restore, clarify, organize and inspire. I can't imagine work without it.

Poetic Exercise: Take a close look at a typical work day. It starts at home, getting ready for work (even if the job is in the home). While no work day (or night) is exactly like every other, look for similarities, breaking your average work day into its component parts: arrival; workspace setup; meetings, visits, and phone calls; writing and answering email; and the parts of the day where you focus on your primary work tasks. Might reading poetry or writing a short poem help breathe life and energy into your day-to-day work? Where could you fit it in?

Try writing a short poem about that bane of modern organizational life—email. It's overwhelming but inescapable. How would you work without email?

Poetry at Work: Airport Security

I'm on my way to San Antonio, standing in the security line at the airport, waiting my turn to deposit my belt, shoes, jacket, wallet and change, laptop and carry-on bag in the plastic bins for X-ray, and then to follow through X-ray myself. This is air travel in 21st century America: herded, X-rayed, peered at, prodded and eventually you get to your destination.

I notice a TSA agent standing in front of the X-ray scanners. He's counting down the line. I look around; no one else notices, too intent on preparing for the security ordeal.

I realize what he's doing. Every eleventh person is being marked for the full pat-down and examination of carry-on bags. I watch him do this with two rows of us lining up. Each time, whoever is eleventh in line is selected for the full security treatment.

He's counting the people in line close to me now, and Number Eleven is directly in front of me. It's a little girl, about six years old. I can actually see the expression on his face change from neutral to almost open dismay. The girl is with her family. She's holding on to a stuffed Mickey Mouse and clutches a pink Cinderella backpack. I heard them talking; they're heading for a family vacation at Disney World.

This Number Eleven is likely to become panicked and reduced to tears. Her parents and siblings will be upset and then outraged. A family vacation is likely to get ruined before it begins.

The agent, a young man, looks at me standing behind the little girl. I nod, and his expression changes again, to relief. In that simple wordless exchange, he knew that I had seen him counting, and he knew that I was saying *take me instead of the little girl*.

It's a small moment in a process repeated millions of times a day. No one has seen this tacit agreement between the two of us.

The TSA agent and I may have written a poem together. A poem about chance—about an event that is both random and methodical, about two people who come together for a brief flash of a moment, who both know they will come away changed.

It is a poem of understanding, an agreement to do something that will substitute a good thing for a potentially bad thing. A child will be spared the agony of a random security search. The agent is doing what he has to do so the TSA and the federal government won't be accused of profiling. We both understand, too, that searching a six-year-old girl probably won't make anyone's airline flight more secure.

And it's a poem of meaning, something that goes deeper than words could convey.

I go through the full pat-down and body scan. My carry-on bags are thoroughly checked. I have to turn my laptop on. The agent himself conducts the check. At the end of it, I hear a whispered "thank you."

I nod again and get my things put back together, and then go to my gate, thinking that I find poetry at work in the most unexpected places.

20

The Poetry of Retirement

Some people find themselves well-situated financially to sail calmly into retirement, but experts say that most of us will need to work longer than our parents did. The reasons mostly have to do with money—or lack of it—due to such issues as the financial disaster of the 2008-2010 recession, lack of personal savings, and being forced to tap into 401K and other savings plans to pay for basic living expenses. Combined, these realities are contributing to a lengthening of the average work life, delaying retirement.

Whenever we reach the end of our career, however, the poetry of work doesn't stop. After all, work is part of every stage of life, so the poetry of work is part of retirement as well.

I'm still a few years from retirement, but close enough to start thinking about it, so when I spent two days visiting my mother in a retirement home not long ago, I approached it differently than I would have ten years earlier. Instead of staying in a hotel and rushing through my time there, I reserved the guest room available to visitors at a relatively low cost that included a one-bedroom apartment and meals with the residents.

Turns out I was something of a celebrity. Few relatives of residents stay that long and that close, and except for the dining room servers, I was the youngest person in the complex. People wanted to meet me, and my mother beamed with the attention. If I were twenty years younger, the slower pace of the retirees and the gushing attention might have left me impatient and antsy. Instead, I listened to them, enjoying the poetry of their life stories.

One man had grown up in the Garden District of New Orleans and talked about the private school he attended in Connecticut. A lady talked about her three husbands: "I can laugh about the first two now, but I couldn't then." Another lady watched every visitor who came into the dining room, hope in her eyes for the family that doesn't seem to come. One woman dressed like a movie star, reminding me of Vanessa Redgrave in the movie *Isadora*. Another lady was a native of France, and as a young girl had married an older American Army general.

I could have written a poem about each person I met; in fact, it's a project I've undertaken.

Having reached a certain age, only fifteen years from some of those residents, I've begun to think about what retirement might look like. I've resolved to continue writing…especially poetry. In fact, I've begun writing poems about the sounds and smells and tastes and travels of a fulfilling retirement, and I'm exploring the lives of my parents.

Before my mother moved to the retirement home, my siblings and I undertook the process we dreaded—breaking up my mother's home, the one she lived in for 58 years. I ended up with photographs I didn't know existed, scrapbooks I had never seen, and pieces that suggest only fragments of their lives. But they are sufficient for creating poetry that both connects and expands the fragments, as I construct narrative from the stories I only know in part and as I recreate the times that came later, writing out stories I remember as a participant in the family activities. That's one of my retirement projects—to make sense of the fragments. Through poetry.

The poetry of work is always unfinished, even when we step away from the workplaces and workspaces where we first began to see poetry come alive in our everyday activities.

I take comfort in that thought. For now, however, I must return to the email that's piling up. A colleague needs some information, and I've got to write a response.

Poetic Exercise: Even if you're years away from retiring, the idea is usually present. You may have experienced your parents' or grandparents' retirement, or the retirement of a much-loved teacher or minister or colleague or someone else who's been important in your life.

Imagine yourself entering retirement. What are you thinking? Have you made financial plans? Do you envision a retirement community or living "someplace warm" like Arizona or Florida? How do your children respond?

Consider each part of a "retired day." Focus on one part, like what you do in the mornings after you wake up and have breakfast. What does the morning look like? What will you be doing? What would you like to be doing? Find the poem in that morning, and write it.

Conclusion

Work is what we all do. We may work for a company, a government agency, a non-profit organization, a school or university, a religious organization, a private foundation, a hospital, or even for ourselves. Regardless of our employer, we work. And poetry can be found in any and all work—not only poetry added on or brought in from the outside, but intrinsically present, waiting for us to realize it, see it, hear it, read it, and write it.

Poetry is part of every aspect of our work experience, from our first job to our last one. Understanding that, for me, has enriched my career, and helped me see both work and poetry in very different ways.

As I mentioned in an earlier chapter, in the mid-1990s I read David Whyte's *The Heart Aroused: Can Poetry Save the Corporate Soul?* The corporate soul was suffering, and David Whyte had an answer—poetry. I don't know if poetry can save the corporate soul, but it can speak deeply to the human souls that comprise it. A few years later, Clare Morgan would offer a practical guide for applying poetry in the workplace, *What Poetry Brings to Business.*

But Whyte and Morgan considered poetry as something distinct from what goes on in the workplace. They brought poetry to work and applied it.

I accepted this idea of poetry as "the other," separate from the business or organizational environment, until I heard the music in that meeting. The music convinced me that poetry was not "the other" when it came to work. It was not something alien to or distinct from work and business, or indeed any kind of work.

Poetry is in work, *it is work*, and it has been there all along.

Recommended Resources

The two best-known prose works that tackle the subject of poetry and work are David Whyte's *The Heart Aroused: Poetry and the Preservation of the Soul in Corporate America* (1994) and Clare Morgan's *What Poetry Brings to Business* (2010). While both focus on business, they're useful for any work setting.

Whyte has also published *Crossing the Unknown Sea: Work as a Pilgrimage of Identity* (2001), which utilizes poetry to explain, enhance, and amplify.

Dana Gioia rocked the poetry world in 1991 with an essay in *The Atlantic* (then known as *The Atlantic Monthly*) on the place of poetry in contemporary culture and followed that up the next year with a collection of essays, *Can Poetry Matter? Essays on Poetry and American Culture.*

In *Beautiful & Pointless: A Guide to Modern Poetry* (2011), David Orr, the poetry columnist for *The New York Times,* provides a succinct summary of what is happening in contemporary poetry.

A suggestion for helping to free your inner poet is *poemcrazy: freeing your life with words* (1997) by Susan Goldsmith Wooldridge. You don't have to do all the suggested exercises—some will cause your neighbors to think you rather odd even if they won't get you arrested—but the book is both fun and inspirational.

Two of the three poets considered the pinnacle of modernist poetry—Wallace Stevens, T. S. Eliot, and Dylan Thomas—were poets and businessmen. Stevens spent his entire working career at the Hartford Insurance Company, and Eliot was a banker. The Library of America has published *Wallace Stevens: Collected Poetry and Prose* (1997), and I have my treasured copy of *The Collected Poems of Wallace Stevens*, first published in 1980. For T. S. Eliot, I strongly recommend *The Complete Poems and Plays: 1909-1950* (published in 1971 but still in print); it's one of my favorite poetry books. (Bear in mind that very few of the poems by Stevens and Eliot deal directly with work.) My edition of *The Poems of Dylan Thomas* was published in 1971 but a revised version was issued in 2003 and includes a CD of Thomas reading eight of his poems.

While it's increasingly difficult to find a traditional bookstore stocking a broad array of poetry books, it's still possible. On a recent vacation in London, I spent some wonderful time browsing the poetry section at Blackwell's on Charing Cross Road; Blackwell's appreciated my time in the shelves, too.

Online, two major resources are The Academy of American Poets at poets.org and the Poetry Foundation at poetryfoundation.org.

And my favorite online poetry site of all—which, among other things, offers a daily inbox delivery of poetry called *Every Day Poems* to help start your work day on a good note,—is *Tweetspeak Poetry* at tweetspeakpoetry.com, the brainchild of L.L. Barkat, founded with the help of friends, including this writer.

Notes

Chapter 1

page 22-23   "By the road to the contagious hospital": William
             Carlos Williams, *Spring and All* (New York: New
             Directions Publishing Co. facsimile edition, 2011),
             Pages 11-12.

Chapter 2

page 30   "Pour the unhappiness out": "Another Weeping
             Woman": Originally published in *Poetry*, October
             1921 (Accessed online at PoetryFoundation.org
             November 2, 2013). <http://www.poetryfounda
             tion.org/poetrymagazine/browse/19/1#!/205732
             57>

Chapter 3

page 35-36   "six actions poets could take to move poetry out
             of academic circles": Dana Gioia, "Can Poetry
             Matter," originally published in *The Atlantic
             Monthly* (now *The Atlantic*) Volume 267, No. 5;
             pages 94-106, March 1991. (Accessed online at
             TheAtlantic.com November 1, 2013)
             <http://www.theatlantic.com/past/docs/un
             bound/poetry/gioia/gioia.htm>

Chapter 4

page 40   "The Strand is beautiful with buses": R.P. Lister,
             "Buses on the Strand" (Accessed online at British-
             Council.org November 1, 2013). <http://litera

ture.britishcouncil.org/projects/2012/poems-on-the-underground>

page 42   "Mrs. Gabrielle Giovannitti comes along Peoria Street every morning": Carl Sandburg "Onion Days" in *Chicago Poems* (New York: Dover Publications, 1994), p. 12.

Chapter 5

page 45   "The poet needs the practicalities of making a living…": David Whyte, *The Heart Aroused: Can Poetry Save the Corporate Soul?* (New York: Double-day, 1994), p. 9.

page 46   "Our lack of soul is our refusal to open…": David Whyte, Ibid, p. 22.

page 46   "the indefinable essence of a person's spirit…": David Whyte, Ibid, p. 13.

page 49   "Precision is vital to a poet …": Clare Morgan, with Kirsten Lange and Ted Buswick, *What Poetry Brings to Business* (Ann Arbor, Michigan: University of Michigan, 2010), p. 13.

Chapter 6

page 56   "Poet of the Great Plains": (Accessed online at PoetryFoundation.org November 1, 2013) <http://www.poetryfoundation.org/bio/ted-kooser>

Chapter 9

page 64   "The creative impulse is essentially innovative":
Luci Shaw, *Breath for the Bones: Art, Imagination and Spirit: A Reflection on Creativity and Faith* (Nashville, TN: Thomas Nelson, 2007), p. 112.

Chapter 11

page 74   "Mark Twain once observed, the most important thing about a speech is knowing when to pause": (Accessed online at twainquotes.com November 3, 2013)<http://www.twainquotes.com/Word.html>

page 75   Gettysburg Address (Accessed online at www.wnyc.org November 12, 2013)<http://www.wnyc.org/story/reciting-gettysburg-address/>

Chapter 12

page 76   "Concreteness makes targets transparent":
Chip Heath and Dan Heath, *Made to Stick: Why Some Ideas Survive and Others Die*, by Chip Heath and Dan Heath, (New York: Random House, 2007), p. 116.

Chapter 16

page 98-99 "Working in a troubled office, you develop":
Robert Cole "October Layoffs": (Accessed online at Richard-Cole.net November 1, 2013; used with permission) <http://richard-cole.net/?p=130>

Chapter 17

page 101　An earlier version of "The Poet Blogs the Layoff" was published at *TheHighCalling.org* <http://www.thehighcalling.org/leadership/ whenlayoffs-and-fear-enter-workplace#.UnVtP_ mTggE>

Chapter 18

page 110　"workaholism is a self-inflicted block on creativity": Julia Cameron, *The Artist's Way: A Spiritual Path to Higher Creativity*, (Accessed Kindle version, Week 10, "Recovering a Sense of Self-Protection, starting at 66 percent).

Acknowledgements

The story of this book is like the story of the Internet—one link leads to another link leads to another link.

One Saturday afternoon in the summer of 2009, a casual conversation on Twitter about the movie *Bottle Crazy* led to the exchange of a few lines of poetry, invented on the spot. And that led to a poetry jam on Twitter that September. And that led to creating a place to post the poems created from the jam, a place called *Tweetspeak Poetry*, which eventually led to an editorial decision to plumb the notion of Poetry at Work and celebrate it with Poetry at Work Day and Take Your Poet to Work Day. So this book owes part of its DNA to an exchange of tweets—thank you, L.L. Barkat and Jim Wood.

No book happens (or should happen) without an editor; Ann Kroeker is one of the best.

Marcus Goodyear gave encouragement when it was needed most, and he didn't even know it.

Three high school English teachers inspired a lifelong love for literature and poetry. How do I thank Joann Roark, Nancy Campbell, and Helen Shorey for that? I can't. But I do anyway.

Friends and colleagues at various places I've worked over the years have lived some of these stories (and some of these "poems") with me: Catharine Vinson, Mary Hadaway, Ron Johnson, John Clifford, Gary Barton, Carl Moskowitz, Susan Fitzgerald, Jim Fullinwider, Scarlett Foster, Diane Herndon, Sajan George, Karen Hylton, Susan Cannon, Scott Stevener, Connie Vivrett, Mark Sutherland, and Chris Paton are only a few I could mention.

My sons, Travis and Andrew, my daughter-in-law, Stephanie, and my two grandsons Cameron and Caden have brought me more joy and inspiration than they'll ever know.

And my wife, Janet, has lived the trials and tribulations of a spouse writing two published novels, seven unpublished novels, and a non-fiction manuscript. She has loved me more than any man has a right to expect.

Also from T. S. Poetry Press

Rumors of Water: Thoughts on Creativity & Writing, by L.L. Barkat

A few brave writers pull back the curtain to show us their creative process. Annie Dillard did this. So did Hemingway. Now L.L. Barkat has given us a thoroughly modern analysis of writing. Practical, yes, but also a gentle uncovering of the art of being a writer.

— Gordon Atkinson, Editor at Laity Lodge

Spin: Taking Your Creativity to the Nth Degree, by Claire Burge

A talisman on your creative journey. It will be your friend for life.

—Mary Carty, author of *50 Monster Ideas*; CEO of Spoiltchild, a BAFTA Nominated Design Agency

The Whipping Club, by Deborah Henry (an Oprah selection)

Multilayered themes of prejudice, corruption and redemption with an authentic voice and swift, seamless dialogue. A powerful saga of love and survival.

—*Kirkus Reviews* (starred review)

Masters in Fine Living Series

The Masters in Fine Living Series is designed to help people live a whole life through the power of reading, writing, and just plain living. Look for titles with the tabs **read, write, live, play, learn,** or **grow**—and join a culture of individuals interested in living deeply, richly.

T. S. Poetry Press titles are available online in e-book and print editions. Print editions also available through Ingram.

tspoetry.com

Made in the USA
Lexington, KY
29 April 2014